# The Refiner's Fire

# The Refiner's Fire

*by*

## *Dr. James H. Correll II*

**Companion Press**
**P.O. Box 310**
**Shippensburg, PA 17257-0310**

"Good Stewards of the
Manifold Grace of God"

ISBN 1-56043-538-0

For Worldwide Distribution
Printed in the U.S.A.

Original cover design by Brenda S. Riddle of Creative Ventures, 4519 Shades Creek Drive, Bessemer, Alabama 35023.

# Contents

# Foreword

Dr. James H. Correll II has explicitly dealt with critical issues that Christians have struggled with for centuries. Included among these are the biblical principles of "predestination" and "why the righteous suffer." He has dealt with these in a direct, straightforward approach. His incisive treatment of these topics, and others, will make you want to read the entire book. One must read *all* to understand *any*. His statement on predestination that, "God's desire is that all mankind might be saved..." is prededicated on the sovereign will of God as well as the free will of man. No one responds to God until, or unless, he is called by the Holy Spirit.

Dr. Correll's treatment of suffering is scriptural and encouraging. God uses suffering to prepare us for a more complete and lasting fellowship with Him. Suffering can be the chastening of God to draw us into a deeper relationship with Him, or it may be used of God to cause us to relent to His Lordship in our lives. God loves us and wants what is best for our lives.

If you are looking for sermonic material or devotional reading, or are searching for some answers to the most complex problems of life, you are apt to find it in *The Refiner's Fire*. God may use it to bless, or change, your life.

Dr. Troy L. Morrison
Executive Secretary-Treasurer
State Board of Missions
Alabama Baptist State Convention

# Introduction

Absolutely helpless. There have only been a few times in my life when I have been at my wit's end and without a clue as to what to do or say.

The first time I remember being at the end of myself was on a Friday night in August, 1964. Sitting on an open wooden bench in the wood shavings of an open-air arbor at the Back to Bethel Campmeeting in China Grove, North Carolina, I was so convicted by the Holy Spirit of my lost and helpless condition before a holy and righteous God that I ran to the altar and begged for mercy. There was nothing to recommend me to God. I was absolutely helpless and a prime candidate for hell, but God saved a 16-year-old boy that night.

There have been other feelings of helplessness through the years. I felt it when ambushed by a North Vietnamese Army unit in 1970 and wounded by shrapnel, far behind enemy lines and dependent on others for air support and extraction from an untenable situation. I feel it upon entering the pulpit on any given Sunday, prepared but seemingly empty and totally dependent upon the Holy Spirit for words, thoughts, and wisdom.

But the most desperate time came on September 28, 1990. Two days earlier, my wife, Dianne, entered my office, sat down in a chair, and started sobbing uncontrollably. In answer to my questions, she informed me her chest was hurting "like a fat woman sitting on it," that her arms were numb, and that this was the third day of that condition. I rushed her to the emergency room and, though the EKG and other tests were inconclusive, she was admitted into the intensive care unit for further tests and observation.

Before dawn on the 28th, she was transferred to a large hospital in Birmingham for a heart catherization "to rule out any heart problem," according to the doctors. The catherization showed a 90 percent blockage of the left anterior descending artery, and the doctors recommended angioplasty be performed that very afternoon to clear the blockage. During the two and one-half hours Dianne was undergoing angioplasty, I knew utter helplessness. I was alone. I paced the floor. I prayed. I questioned the lady at the desk. I fretted. I begged God not to let her die. Yes, I knew she was in competent hands. Yes, I knew God would take care of her. But I also knew there was not one physical thing I could do to influence the outcome, and I felt helpless.

It is one thing to tell others that God loves them and works all things out for their good, but it is another thing altogether to accept it for yourself. The procedure was successful, and Dianne is again healthy. God did come through, as he always does. But he chose to preserve her through the trial, not from it.

This book was born out of a desire to help Christians who suffer and wonder why. What is God up to, anyway? Would a good God really let his children suffer? The popular myth making the rounds today is that Christians with real faith need never suffer. Is that what the Bible teaches? Can I as a pastor truthfully tell someone devastated by cancer that his condition is caused only by a lack of faith? It's time to tell people the truth, and that I have attempted to do.

This book is based solely on biblical principles and examines how God uses trials to enrich the lives of his children on earth and to prepare them for heaven. My study shows that suffering among believers is to be expected and that God uses it to conform us to the image of Christ, to test our faith for purity, and to draw us closer to him in identity, joy, love, and trust. The situations are not contrived but are the stories of real people facing real problems in a real world. I believe this work meets a pressing need in a society besieged with superficial answers to complex problems.

I wanted to tell people the truth about suffering, but I was concerned that I was an outsider, never having experienced much suffering myself. Maybe that's why Dianne got sick. Maybe, just maybe, God wanted to let me test him and his Word in a crisis. Maybe you'll believe me when I tell you that God's grace is sufficient for every trial in the crucible of your life.

# Chapter 1

# Conformed to the Image of Christ

In the storm of the emergency room, Billie Oswalt sought refuge and found it for a time in her thoughts. The events of the past hour or so exceeded her greatest fears and flooded her mind. Was this a dream? Had it really happened?

Returning in mid-afternoon from a bridal tea, she had casually walked down toward the pasture to let her husband know she was home. As she approached the fence, she heard a faint, "Help!" and her blood turned cold. Her husband lay unmoving under a tree limb which had struck him on the back of the head as he tried to cut a fallen tree off the fence. Paralyzed. Praying. Three hours he had waited.

She ran for help. The neighbors came, followed in minutes by the paramedics. After what seemed like an eternity, the Life Saver helicopter arrived and departed to airlift her most cherished possession away, perhaps forever.

"Billie. Billie." She was startled out of her reverie by the sound of her name being called. It was her pastor. She had been surprised to find him already at the hospital when she arrived. How did he get there so fast on such a rainy day? He was calling her name again.

"Billie, you know you would not have been able to handle this at all a year and a half ago."

It was true, A diabetic, she had more than two years earlier stubbed her toe, and it had never healed. A mere eighteen months ago the bone specialist had shocked her with the assessment that she would "lose the toe, perhaps the foot, maybe part of the leg." For the first time in her life, she had known sheer panic. She cried day and night and asked God a thousand times, "Why?"

In the ensuing year, the doctors had tried many procedures, but the decision had finally been made to remove a third of her foot. When the time for the amputation came, however, there was no panic. In that year she had grown so much in the Lord that she could honestly say, "Whatever the Lord wills in my life is okay with me. I know he will take care of me. I am not afraid."

Now she was the picture of calm as her world seemingly crashed around her. Now she was trusting her husband to the Lord's care. Now she was steadfast in her faith.

What had happened? What was it that had brought her from a whimpering, self-centered, panic-stricken baby Christian a year and a half ago to a confident, God-trusting, rock of serenity today?

God, knowing all things and knowing the end from the beginning, had prepared her for this crisis by conforming her to the image of his Son: "For whom he did foreknow, he also did predestinate to be conformed to the image of his Son" (Rom. 8:29). Now she could agree with the Apostle Paul when he wrote, "And we know that all things work together for good to them that love God, to them who are the called according to his purpose" (Rom. 8:28). All that had happened had been for a purpose, and the purpose was now clear. God was conforming her to the image of Jesus Christ.

## Total Obedience

Just what is the image of God's Son to which believers are predestined? It is undoubtedly one of absolute and total obedience.

When asked by his disciples to teach them to pray, Jesus told them to ask God the Father for his unrestricted will in their lives: "Thy kingdom come. Thy will be done, as in heaven, so in earth" (Luke 11:2). In the portals of heaven, God's will is obeyed without question or hesitation.

In the garden the night before his death, Jesus cried to the Father, "Not my will, but thine be done" (Luke 22:42). Jesus was obedient even unto death, and believers are predestined to be conformed to his image.

Jesus warned his disciples that they must make a choice between family and him. To follow him, he said, requires one to bear a "cross" of his own:

*If any man come to me, and hate not his father, and mother, and wife, and children, and brethren, and sisters, yea, and his own life also, he cannot be my disciple. And whosoever doth not bear his cross, and come after me, cannot be my disciple.*

Luke 14:26-27

J. Dwight Pentecost has correctly observed that

The cross in the life of Christ was the test of His obedience to the will of God. The cross was to Christ what the tree of the knowledge of good and evil was to Adam in the Garden of Eden. Christ was saying that His disciples must not only choose to follow Him and commit themselves to His headship, but they also must submit themselves to His will. Insisting on one's own will and claiming the right to one's own life exclude one from being a disciple of Christ.[1]

## The Conforming Process

How does God go about conforming his children to the image of his only begotten Son? What is his process?

At the outset, we must understand that Romans 8:28-30 has no meaning for the unsaved. It cannot be said that anything works together for good to the lost, because they are unrighteous, and nothing they do can ever be considered to be good until they are declared righteous by God in justification. While all deserved to be separated from God for eternity, no one is forced to be lost. The lost have chosen to be lost. The unbeliever is not predestined, called, justified, or glorified, and he is certainly not being conformed to the image of Jesus Christ.

The believer, on the other hand, is said to be all of these, as well as foreknown. Foreknowledge is not just advanced knowledge but God bringing to

---

1.    J. Dwight Pentecost, *The Parables of Jesus* (Grand Rapids: Zondervan Publishing House, 1982), 96-97.

pass that which he planned. God knew, sanctified, and ordained Jeremiah before he was ever born (Jer. 1:4-5), and Paul says that believers were chosen before the creation of the world to be "holy and without blame before him in love" (Eph. 1:4). God clearly made choices before the first man or the world was ever created. Knowing man would rebel against his authority, God decided to save and conform some. The age-old question remains this: Did God choose because he foreknew, or did he foreknow because he chose? Whether you prefer the former or the latter, only in eternity will we really understand the mind of God in this matter. The mind of man is not sufficient to reconcile these things. And the opinion of man changes nothing.

I have always been amused by the bumper sticker which reads, "God said it, I believe it, that settles it." The only problem with that is that it is wrong. If God said it, that settles it, whether I believe it or not. And man's opinion about God's thought processes in foreknowing and choosing makes no difference. He did it the way he wanted.

## Predestination

The first step in the conforming process, then, is predestination. Nothing stirs the emotions quite like the word "predestination." It is an explosive word. It is a misunderstood concept, largely because most people do not comprehend the goal of predestination. What is the goal of predestination? Sanctification. When one is ultimately and completely sanctified, brought from filthy to lovely, then he has been conformed to the image of God's Son—"For whom he did foreknow, he also did predestinate to be conformed to the image of his Son, that he might be the firstborn among many brethren" (Rom. 8:29).

Those who reject the sovereignty of God will never accept the concept of predestination or election, but those who understand his sovereignty will see predestination as a precious assurance of position in Christ. The Greek word (*proorisen*) translated "did predestinate" in Romans 8:29 is in the aorist tense, indicating a completed action in the past.[2] In other words, God had a plan, and in his plan he foreordained that some would be conformed to the image of his beloved Son. He chose some, not all.

Someone always objects at this point that because God made choices he predestined some to be lost and to go to hell. Not so. The lost have chosen to be lost. No one is forced to be lost. All deserved to be separated from God forever, and, left to his own devices, not one person would ever be saved

2. Fritz Rienecker, *Linguistic Key to the Greek New Testament*, ed. Cleon L. Rogers, Jr. (Grand Rapids: Zondervan Publishing House, 1980), 367.

because he has a sinful and rebellious nature. In spite of his justice and man's sin, however, God decided to take some to heaven in spite of themselves. The impulse for salvation begins with God, not man. No one responds to the gospel until he has been quickened by the Holy Spirit. Does God quicken everyone? I'm not sure he does, but I am sure he is fair. I'm amazed he chose to save anybody, given man's rebellion and depravity. Sovereign God has the right to decide, and he has exercised that right.

I believe James Kennedy's bank robbery analogy comes very close to clarifying God's elective actions:

Here are five people who are planning to hold up a bank. They are friends of mine. I find out about it and I plead with them not to do it. Finally they push me out of the way and they start out. I tackle one of the men and wrestle him to the ground. The others go ahead, rob the bank, a guard is killed, they are captured, convicted, sentenced to the electric chair, and die. The one man who was not involved in the robbery goes free. Now I ask you this question: Whose fault was it that these other men died? Did I make them hold up the bank? Did I encourage them to do it? Did I cause them to do it? Did I urge them to do it? Or did I plead with them not to do it? Was it not their own free choice of their own sinful hearts, their own cupidity, their own lust for money, that caused them to do it? They had nobody to blame but themselves. Now this other man who is walking around free—can he say, "Because my heart is so good, I am a free man?" The only reason that he is free is because of me; because I restrained him. So those who go to hell *have no one to blame but themselves.* Those who go to heaven *have no one to praise but Jesus Christ.* Thus we see that salvation is *all of grace,* from its beginning to its end. It is all of God. He is the one that seeks us and draws us unto himself.[3]

Since sin's inception, man has tried to blame God, but God is not to blame. Paul posed the question, "Is there unrighteousness with God?" and answered with a resounding, "God forbid" (Rom. 9:14). God is righteous, and he has reasons for doing things that we cannot understand. Jesus said, "What I do thou knowest not now; but thou shalt know hereafter" (John 13:7). Abraham, Isaac, and Jacob all deserved hell, but God chose to glorify himself through them and the nation of Israel. Does this make God unfair? Absolutely not! If God were totally fair, all would be lost. Man does

---

3.  D. James Kennedy, *Truths That Transform* (Old Tappan, New Jersey: Fleming H. Revell Company, 1974), 35.

not really want God's justice, despite his protestations that God is not fair. Justice means hell for all. It is God's universe, and he does not have to show mercy or compassion on anyone or everyone. The fact that he has chosen some to be recipients of his mercy and grace is evidence of his love for mankind.

Someone may say that salvation is for "whosoever will," and that is true. But God's mercy is not generated or extended because of human will or work:

> *He came unto his own, and his own received him not. But as many as received him, to them gave he power to become the sons of God, even to them that believe on his name: Which were born, not of blood, nor of the will of the flesh, nor of the will of man, but of God.*

> John 1:11-13

Human will is not a factor. The *chosen* nation Israel was told, "Choose you this day whom ye will serve" (Josh. 24:15). In the New Testament, we read, "And whosoever will, let him take of the water of life freely" (Rev. 22:17). To will is to determine, and nobody will come, nobody will determine to accept Christ of himself. As a matter of fact, the whole "whosoever will" concept only proves man's depravity and incapability to come to God and God's great mercy and grace in saving man. The concept also gives assurance of eternal life to the believer, because he believes what the carnal mind cannot, having been quickened by the Holy Spirit.

Time after time in the Book of Exodus we read that "Pharaoh hardened his heart" or "the LORD hardened Pharaoh's heart." What does this mean? It simply means that God caused Pharaoh to make the decision that was in his heart. Was God righteous in not softening Pharaoh's heart? Yes. Pharaoh did what he wanted to do. The wonder is that God softens anyone's heart.

When we understand that God, as Creator, is the Potter and has the right to do with the clay as he wishes, we can better accept election. The clay has no complaint. God could have destroyed Pharaoh at his first refusal, could have cut off Israel over the golden calf, and could have cut off humanity forever in Adam, but he is merciful (Rom. 9:22-23). The clay deserves nothing, and God's choice of Israel, his choice to save Gentiles, and his choice to save individuals are but manifestations of his power, glory, and mercy. He works according to the good pleasure of his own will, and the clay has no right to complain. The prophet Jeremiah explains:

*The word which came to Jeremiah from the LORD, saying, Arise and go down to the potter's house, and there I will cause thee to hear my words. Then I went down to the*

*potter's house, and, behold, he wrought a
work on the wheels. And the vessel that he
made of clay was marred in the hand of the
potter: so he made it again another vessel, as
seemed good to the potter to make it. Then the
word of the LORD came to me, saying, O
house of Israel, cannot I do with you as this
potter? saith the LORD. Behold, as the clay is
in the potter's hand, so are ye in mine hand, O
house of Israel.*

Jer. 18:1-6

Men who reject God's sovereignty still ask, "If
God makes the choices, how can he hold man
responsible, and who can resist his decision?" We
must answer that men are lost because they rebel
against God's light and truth, not because God has
chosen them to be lost. Jesus said that men are
rebellious, not ignorant.

*And this is the condemnation, that light is
come into the world, and men loved darkness
rather than light, because their deeds were
evil. For every one that doeth evil hateth the
light, neither cometh to the light, lest his
deeds should be reproved. But he that doeth
truth cometh to the light, that his deeds may
be manifest, that they are wrought of God.*

John 3:19-21

Why does God find fault with man? Because man is
at fault. God alone is wisdom and alone is capable

of deciding what is best for his universe. God has never asked for my advice. He does not need to consult man or Satan, because neither can ever be God, though both will certainly try.

Then why not "let nature take its course," since those elected will surely make it to heaven, Jesus himself affirming they have eternal life (John 17:2)? Simply because the witness does not know who is predestined; because he has been given a commandment to go, teach, and baptize (Matt. 28:18-20); and because no one can believe without hearing (Rom. 10:14). Election is for the saved, not the lost. In the Book of Romans, Paul shows man his depravity and need of a Savior long before he ever mentions election as a means of assuring saints their salvation can never be lost. Knowing his position in Christ is secure, a believer is better equipped to witness to others of God's amazing grace. I bear witness to a saving *and* keeping God.

Predestination exists. God has chosen to save some in spite of themselves. Jesus died for "whosoever believeth in him" (John 3:16). Only those quickened will believe, because "there is none that understandeth, there is none that seeketh after God" (Rom. 3:11). It is only by God's mercy and grace that any are saved. Predestination is a problem only to the finite mind of man, not to the infinite mind of God. We'll understand it better by and by.

## Calling

Step number two is calling—"Moreover, whom he did predestinate, them he also called" (Rom. 8:30). To be called is "more than being invited to receive Christ; it means to be summoned to and given salvation."[4] A dead sinner is incapable of responding to God until he is quickened and implanted with faith. God clearly took the initiative in reconciling mankind to himself. Left to his own devices, not one man would ever have responded to God because of the sinful nature with which he was born. John declared in his first epistle, "We love him, because he first loved us" (1 John 4:19), and "Herein is love, not that we loved God, but that he loved us, and sent his Son to be the propitiation for our sins" (1 John 4:10). God did it all, and he did it first. For any man to attempt to take any credit for salvation or the conforming process is rather absurd.

Many today want to take credit for finding God. Many wrongly claim to have "sought" God and "found" him. It is amazing to find that God was lost in the first place. Such a concept denies clear biblical teaching that "there is none that seeketh after God" (Rom. 3:11). Can anyone honestly picture

---

4.    John F. Walvoord and Roy B. Zuck, *The Bible Knowledge Commentary*, New Testament edition (Wheaton: Victor Books, 1983), 474.

those "who were dead in trespasses and sins" (Eph. 2:1) seeking God, calling on him, or finding him without first being quickened? God does the calling.

## Justification

The third step is justification—"and whom he called, them he also justified" (Rom. 8:30). Answering the call in the heart results in justification. What is justification? It is the act whereby God declares the ungodly righteous and counts him as perfect in Christ. God records in heaven that one whom he has chosen previously for salvation and conformity to Christ has been effectually called and is no longer dead in trespasses and sin but is alive through redemption. Declared righteous by God—that is justification.

A literal reading of Romans 3:23 shows just how hopeless man is without God: "All sinned (aorist tense, at a point of time in the past, i.e., in Adam) and keep on falling short (present tense) of the glory of God."[5] No matter what we think, no matter our religious ideas, no matter if we reject sin as a false concept of someone's mind, this verse clearly states that because of our forefather, Adam, and because of our own imperfections, we are bankrupt

---

5.  Walvoord and Zuck, *Bible Knowledge Commentary*, New Testament edition, 450-451.

before God and have a death sentence upon our heads (Rom. 5:12; 6:23). God declares that men are lost sinners.

In justification, however, God declares the believing sinner righteous, as if he had never sinned at all. This is more than forgiveness, which removes the penalty but not the guilt. It is more than pardon, which likewise cannot remove guilt. It is more than cleansing. It is being declared righteous by God's decree. The tense in Romans 3:24 indicates that it keeps on happening, covering life past, present, and future, and it is a free gift: "Being justified freely by his grace through the redemption that is in Christ Jesus." God gave heaven to men who deserved hell by declaring them righteous without cause found in them at all.

## Glorification

Glorification is the fourth step in the process of being conformed to the image of Christ—"and whom he justified, them he also glorified" (Rom. 8:30). What an assuring statement. This is another way of saying that all of God's children will be ultimately conformed to the image of Christ, which is God's purpose in their lives. "Glorified" is written in the past tense, prophetically signifying that it is as good as done in God's sight. He sees the believer as already in heaven. In his excellent commentary on the Book of Romans, Donald Grey Barnhouse has made this observation concerning glorification:

God is flatly stating that He already looks upon us, sinful creatures though we may be, as though we were now in Heaven. Moreover, He has thus looked upon us from all eternity.[6]

Or, as Warren Wiersbe has expressed,

We are just as much glorified as we are justified, *but the glory has not yet been revealed.* All of creation, now travailing because of sin, is eagerly awaiting "the revealing of the sons of God" (Romans 8:19); for only then will creation be set free to enjoy "the freedom of the glory of the children of God" (Romans 8:21).[7]

Believers do not have to live their lives in suspense, wondering if they will make it to heaven or not. God sees them as already there, glorified like Jesus. What a wonderful thought! Not a single believer can ever be lost, because God has seen him in heaven since before the world was created. "Heirs of God, and joint-heirs with Christ" (Rom. 8:17), believers are even now positionally at the right hand of the Father, in the position of

---

6. Donald Grey Barnhouse, *Romans*, 4 vols. (Grand Rapids: William B. Eerdmans Publishing Company, 1952-1960), 3:174.

7. Warren W. Wiersbe, *Prayer: Basic Training* (Wheaton, Illinois: Tyndale House Publishers, 1982), 30.

authority with Christ. Fanny Crosby said it exactly right:

> Blessed assurance, Jesus is mine!
> Oh, what a foretaste of glory divine!
> Heir of salvation, purchase of God.
> Born of his Spirit, wash'd in his blood.[8]

## Conformity

The final step is conformity. To this believers are predestined. God's ultimate purpose is that believers be conformed finally and completely to the image of Christ, not just his image as he walked this earth in humanity but to his glorified image on his throne.

*Beloved, now are we the sons of God, and it doth not yet appear what we shall be: but we know that, when he shall appear, we shall be like him; for we shall see him as he is.*

1 John 3:2

Predestined for the throne. Headed for the throne. Bound for heaven with no possibility of detour or abort. Guaranteed arrival for all believers. Predestination should not be frightening but thrilling, because God cannot lose a single one

8.   Fanny Crosby, "Blessed Assurance, Jesus Is Mine" (written 1873), *Baptist Hymnal* (Nashville: Convention Press, 1975), 334.

of his own. Those who have been saved will be conformed to the image of God's Son and will arrive safely in heaven. Those who have never been saved and want to, can be. The very desire to be saved is from the Holy Spirit. God's desire is that all mankind might be saved, "not willing that any should perish, but that all should come to repentance" (2 Pet. 3:9). For this he sent his Son, and for the image of his Son believers are predestined.

## Extended Suffering

Why is it that some believers suffer for such a long time while others suffer hardly at all? Why does one man in a church get sick one day and die the next? How can God be fair and allow a man to contract a seemingly innocent ailment such as influenza and die two weeks later with acute leukemia? Why did Billie have to suffer for such a long time only to see her husband struck down with a paralysis that has not yet been completely overcome? What is God up to by allowing some of his children to suffer so long?

Obviously, no one has all the answers. While there is but one way to salvation, and that Jesus Christ crucified and risen again (John 14:6), there are as many paths from the cross to heaven as there are believers. The wonder of the body of Christ, the church, is that every member is not only different but unique. And, in some cases, believers suffer for extended periods of time because they are being conformed to the image of Jesus Christ and because they would never be conformed in any other way.

In his great prayer of intercession, Jesus indicated that his mission on the earth was to glorify the Father. He prayed, "I have glorified thee on the earth: I have finished the work which thou gavest me to do" (John 17:4). David Ring, an evangelist born with cerebral palsy, says that our proper response to suffering is not, "Why?", but "What? What can I do or become to glorify God in the pain? Asking 'Why?' questions God's authority, forms bitterness in our lives, and makes us come up empty every time as we look only at our circumstances."[9]

If every believer is to be conformed to the image of Christ, and the mission of Christ here on the earth was to glorify the Father, then it seems reasonable to constantly ask the question, "What can I do or become to glorify God in this pain?"

One of the most remarkable statements made about any man is found in Romans 4:3—"Abraham believed God, and it was counted unto him for righteousness." Abraham believed God and was

---

9.   Message delivered November 13, 1989, at Whitesburg Baptist Church, Huntsville, Alabama. From personal notes of the author.

called the friend of God. What was it about Abraham that made him the friend of God? He believed God. And the stories of the great men and women of the Bible have one thing in common: they believed God. Chapter eleven of Hebrews is full of the names of many who walked by faith. They believed God.

Now, every Christian must believe God for his salvation. Recognizing his lost condition, his hopelessness to save himself, and his need of a Savior, he believes God and trusts Jesus Christ, God's only begotten Son, as his Savior. Sadly, however, that is the last time many Christians find a reason to believe God until some tragedy strikes. God wants to be believed! He wants those who have trusted him for their salvation and their eternity to trust him with their daily lives. He wants them to walk by faith. He wants their total obedience and confidence. He wants them to be like Jesus.

To this end, God sometimes has to bring extended suffering into the life of a believer. The believer must come to understand that *all* things are working together for his good. Abel speaks louder in death than he ever would have in life. Job was refined in the loss of material things. The sin of Naomi's son in marrying a Moabitess (Deut. 7:1-4; 23:3) brought Ruth into God's fold. Joseph told his brothers the evil they thought against him was meant unto good by God (Gen. 50:20). Satan intended the death of Christ as the ultimate attack on God, but God turned it into salvation from sin for multitudes of people. The believer's lack of understanding of a period of suffering in his life in no way changes the truth, and the truth is that even extended suffering is working to his eventual good. For, as Philip Yancey has written,

> The Bible clearly demonstrates that some things are more awful to God than the pain of his children. Consider the psychological pain Abraham underwent when God asked him to kill his son Isaac. Or the awesome pain of Himself becoming man and bearing the sins of the world. Skeptics have cited these incidents as examples of God's lack of compassion. To me, they prove that some things —like declaring the truth—are more important on God's agenda than the suffering-free world for even His most loyal followers.[10]

The conformity of believers to the image of Christ is certainly one of those things which is more important to God than the suffering of his children. Those who will not trust him, who refuse to walk by faith, are asking God to bring suffering into their lives. Inadvertently, to be sure, but that is the message they send. The purpose of predestination was not justification, but sanctification,

---

10. Philip Yancey, *Where Is God When It Hurts* (Grand Rapids: Zondervan Publishing House, 1977), 55.

daily holy living. That is a lifestyle that is not attainable without the leadership of the Holy Spirit. Paul described his attempt to live a holy life in the absence of the filling of the Spirit as "wretched" (Rom. 7:24). It was only when he began to "walk not after the flesh, but after the Spirit" (Rom. 8:4) that he could grasp that in Christ Jesus there was no condemnation, no separation, and all things worked together for good.

So it is with the believer today. Walking out of the fullness of the Spirit, not trusting God to lead him in a holy walk, and refusing obedience to God, he is not being conformed to the image of Christ. But he will be conformed, one way or the other, because that is his destiny. Why do so many make it so hard on themselves?

One more thing needs to be said on this subject. Christ is seated on the throne of God and will one day be returning to this earth as "KING OF KINGS AND LORD OF LORDS" (Rev. 19:16). Saints are to "reign with him a thousand years" (Rev. 10:6). Part of the conforming process on the earth for believers is obviously a preparation for the exercise of government in the millennial kingdom. To reign with Christ not only requires that the believer trust God implicitly, but that God trust the believer in any given situation. As the parables of Christ clearly indicate, those who have been faithful in a few things will be made rulers over many. A believer is not ready to reign until he has been conformed to the image of Christ, and he is not truly conformed to the image of Christ until he is totally obedient, totally trusting, and totally committed to the glory of God the Father.

Why do some suffer for a long time? In some cases, it is because they refuse to be conformed willingly to the image of God's Son, and God has to bring suffering to mold them. That is their destiny.

# Chapter 2

# Yielded to God's Will

"Since I've been with the Lord in total surrender, I'll never be happy again to be just a Christian."

I sat stunned, unbelieving, as the voice from the cassette tape recorder fell silent. As if in a daze, I pressed the rewind button and then started the tape again. The message was the same: "Since I've been with the Lord in total surrender, I'll never be happy again to be just a Christian."

I had not known that such depth existed in any of my people. Yet here was one who had known the horror of cancer testifying that it was the experience of cancer that brought her to a state of absolute surrender to the lordship of Jesus Christ, and that she would never again be happy as "just a Christian" now that she had known the joy of being yielded to her Lord.

Kaye Bailey was saved April 12, 1950, but was a "marginal Christian" for 36 years. It was in November 1986 that the doctors discovered she had lymphoma, cancer of the lymph glands. For the next six months she took massive doses of chemotherapy. She tried to continue her work as manager of a school lunch room, but she found herself weak and exhausted after only one hour of work. Finally, after four months of treatments, she had to go home early one day because she was so weak. Leaving the school in tears, she hit the bottom emotionally. She felt God had forsaken her, that he had let her down. For the first time in her life, she knew what it meant to be angry at God.

Upon arriving home, she discovered an envelope addressed to her in her capacity as lunch room manager, but the contents, obviously intended for someone else but supernaturally rerouted by God to one of his children in need, were anything but official. Wrapped in a plain white sheet of paper was this poem by an unknown author:

*I asked for strength that I might achieve;*
*He made me weak that I might obey.*

*I asked for health that I might do greater
    things;
I was given grace that I might do better things.
I asked for riches that I might be happy;
I was given poverty that I might be wise.
I asked for power that I might have the praise
    of men;
I was given weakness that I might feel the need
    of God.
I asked for all things that I might enjoy life;
I was given life that I might enjoy all things.
I received nothing that I asked for, all that I
    hoped for;
My prayer was answered.*

Kaye was convinced to the end that her receipt of this poem was a miracle. But her troubles were far from over. The cancer came back a year and a half later. She fell into deep depression and one night awoke from a dream about cancer absolutely terrified. To calm her fears, she started praying and heard a voice say, "Leave it with me." The next day was Sunday, and Kaye went to the altar and poured out her heart to God: "God, please take this burden from me. I can't handle this. I'm giving all this to you." She heard a second voice say, "Don't pick it up again."

The tests showed that the lump in her neck was indeed cancer. As she underwent intense chemotherapy treatments once again, coupled with radiation treatments this time, she experienced a calmness and peace she never knew before.

Why did Kaye Bailey have to endure not one but two bouts with cancer? Perhaps her own analysis is best: "If it weren't so terrible, I'd thank God for cancer. It showed me how weak I am, and I have to depend on God's strength to get me through each day. My prayer is that God's grace will cover me throughout the rest of my life, and that whatever comes, I'll be able to show the world that I'm a Christian, totally dependent on God." And then she concluded her testimony with that remarkable thought, "Since I've been with God in total surrender, I'll never be happy again to be just a Christian."

## A Question of Lordship

What was it that brought Kaye Bailey to the point of total surrender and dependence on God? What vaulted her after 36 years from the earthbound steps of marginal Christianity to the eagle's flight of Christian maturity? It was suffering. Sadly, her story is not the exception, because many believers, if not most, never yield to the lordship of Jesus Christ except in suffering.

This is not to say that a believer has never yielded and acknowledged Christ's lordship, for it is only when a lost sinner recognizes his hopelessness, his bankruptcy outside of Jesus Christ that he can be saved. The New Testament six times identifies Christ as Savior and Lord in the same verse (1 Tim. 1:1; Titus 1:4; 2 Pet. 1:11; 2:20; 3:2, 18). So in trusting Christ to be his Savior, a sinner who would be saved must also accept him as Lord and Master.

The problem comes after salvation in the normal day-to-day life of most Christians because, although Jesus Christ is indeed the Lord, he is not really Lord in the life of any believer until that believer commits his entire life to Christ and obeys him totally. The Bible makes it very clear that the scope, or realm, of his lordship is universal, as Philippians 2:9-11 describes:

*Wherefore God also hath highly exalted him, and given him a name which is above every name: That at the name of Jesus every knee should bow, of things in heaven, and things in earth, and things under the earth; And that every tongue should confess that Jesus Christ is Lord, to the glory of God the Father.*

John 1:1-3 and Colossians 1:15-16 identify him as Lord of creation. Colossians 1:18 pictures him as Lord of the church. In Revelation 19:16, he is seen as Lord of all authorities, "KING OF KINGS AND LORD OF LORDS." Revelation 14:11 presents him as Lord of every facet of life. He is Lord over everyone and everything, and all must acknowledge his lordship one day. Since we do not have many lords and masters today, it is sometimes hard for us to grasp just what lordship means. I think the best way to express it in today's terms is that Jesus is Boss. Everyone knows what a boss is, and Jesus wants to be Boss in the lives of his children. Lord, Master, Boss. This is what Jesus wants to be and should be in my life.

The question then is not, "Is he *the* Lord?" He is *the* Lord. The question is, however, "Is he *my* Lord?" He cannot be part Lord—it is all or nothing. Many have observed, "If he is not Lord of all, he is not Lord at all." And each believer must decide daily who will be on the throne in his life. Will it be Christ, self, or someone else? Christ is not Lord in a life unless he is reigning in a life.

How, then, may we judge whether Christ is really Lord of our lives? How can we know if the lordship of Christ is more than just a claim, a profession from the lips, or the words of a hymn? Charles Stanley offers eight principles by which we may take a spiritual inventory:

1. Jesus Christ is my Lord when I obey the initial promptings of the Holy Spirit without hesitation or argument...
2. Jesus Christ is my Lord when I am committed to fulfilling His will for my life before I even know what he will require of me.

3. Jesus Christ is my Lord when I am available to serve him without regard to time, space, or circumstances.

4. Jesus Christ is my Lord when I recognize His ownership of my total life and all of my possessions—and submit to that ownership.

5. Jesus Christ is my Lord when pleasing Him exceeds my desire to please others...

6. Jesus Christ is my Lord when I look to Him as the source of all my needs and desires...

7. Jesus Christ is my Lord when I am turning my difficulties and my failures into opportunities for spiritual growth...

8. Jesus Christ is my Lord when to know Him intimately becomes the obsession of my life.[1]

Andrew Murray says that any believer can make Jesus Christ his Lord by giving the Lord his place, accepting his will in everything, trusting his almighty power, and sacrificing everything for him.[2] Stanley, too, emphasizes commitment and obedience: "It is not enough to call Him Lord. He is King of kings and Lord of lords, whether or not you are committed and obedient to Him."[3]

1. Charles Stanley, *Confronting Casual Christianity* (Nashville: Broadman Press, 1985), 164-166.
2. Andrew Murray, *The Believer's Absolute Surrender* (Minneapolis: Bethany House Publishers, 1985), 48-53.
3. Stanley, *Confronting Casual Christianity*, 167.

When the Lord allows suffering to come into the lives of his children, then, it may be that he is bringing them to a position where they, like Kaye Bailey, are forced to acknowledge their helplessness and to surrender their lives to God's will. Millions would testify that they never obeyed the imperative, "Be filled with the Spirit" (Eph. 5:18) nor lived the Spirit-filled life until brought to their knees in some trial. What pastor has not agreed with Dwight L. Moody that he could turn his town upside down for Christ with just a handful of Christians sold out for the Lord? And yet where are the towns, cities, or countries where true revival is taking place? It seems they do not exist today. Is it any wonder that God allows suffering to come as a means of correcting complacency and apathy among the redeemed? The Lord of the universe wants to be the Lord in the life of every believer, and he will bring suffering, if necessary, to establish lordship in a Christian's life. His lordship is more important than the believer's health.

## Preparation for Heaven

Luke records in his Gospel that the disciples on one occasion asked Jesus to teach them to pray (Luke 11:1). Matthew recalls that this happened during the Sermon on the Mount, when Jesus gave his disciples the following model prayer:

*After this manner therefore pray ye: Our Father which art in heaven, Hallowed be thy name. Thy kingdom come. Thy will be done in earth, as it is in heaven. Give us this day our daily bread. And forgive us our debts, as we forgive our debtors. And lead us not into temptation, but deliver us from evil: For thine is the kingdom, and the power, and the glory, for ever. Amen.*

Matt. 6:9-13

Volumes have been written on this prayer, but some things are particularly striking, including ascribing glory to God the Father; asking for daily provisions, forgiveness of sins, and deliverance from evil; and a final acknowledgement that all majesty, power, and glory belong to God.

The most striking parts of the prayer, however, are the simple statements, "Thy kingdom come. Thy will be done in earth, as it is in heaven." For in voicing this plea, the believer is not only looking for the day when Christ will return in power and glory to establish his millennial "kingdom" on the earth, but he is also asking that God prepare him for heaven. In heaven, God's will is done. Period. End of discussion. There was only one will in the universe until Lucifer said, "I will," as Isaiah records:

*For thou hast said in thine heart, I will ascend into heaven, I will exalt my throne above the stars of God: I will sit also upon the mount of the congregation, in the sides of the north: I will ascend above the heights of the clouds; I will be like the most High.*

Isa. 14:13-14

God immediately pronounced judgment, not mercy or grace, upon him by declaring him "fallen from heaven" (Isa. 14:12) and destined for "hell, to the sides of the pit" (Isa. 14:15). John saw the eventual destiny of Lucifer, who had been a beautiful cherub (Ezek. 28:13-17), as the lake of fire for eternity:

*And the devil that deceived them was cast into the lake of fire and brimstone, where the beast and the false prophet are, and shall be tormented day and night for ever and ever.*

Rev. 20:10

"Thy will be done in earth, as it is in heaven," the disciples were taught to pray. "Lord, do whatever you have to do to bring us to the point where your will is the only thing that matters to us in this earth. May your will be so important to us that your will becomes our will. May we never desire anything that is not in accordance with your will. May your will be as absolute in our lives as it is in heaven. Lord, prepare us for heaven." That is what the Lord taught his disciples to pray. That also should be the prayer of every believer today.

But yielding to the will of God is not easy. As a matter of fact, it is so opposed to human nature that it is probably the most difficult thing anyone ever does. To be prepared for heaven, however, "self" must take a back seat. Stanley puts it this way:

God is not satisfied with well-mannered, respectable "self" on the throne of our lives. He wants to remove all traces of "self" so that we can be presented to Christ holy and blameless. One way God accomplishes that is by sending adversity into our lives. Adversity stirs us up and causes us to look at life differently. We are forced to deal with things on a deeper level. Nothing causes "self" to cave in like suffering. And once our religious facade begins to wear thin, God moves in and begins teaching us what real Christlikeness is all about.[4]

Paul describes the process as a crucifixion of the old self:

*I am crucified with Christ: nevertheless I live; yet not I, but Christ liveth in me: and the life which I now live in the flesh I live by the faith of the Son of God, who loved me, and gave himself for me.*

Gal. 2:20

---

4. Charles Stanley, *How to Handle Adversity* (Nashville: Thomas Nelson Publishers, 1989), 156.

And again in Romans 6:3-7:

*Know ye not, that so many of us as were bap-
tized into Jesus Christ were baptized into his
death? Therefore we are buried with him by
baptism unto death: that like as Christ was
raised up from the dead by the glory of the
Father, even so we also should walk in new-
ness of life. For if we have been planted
together in the likeness of his death, we shall
be also in the likeness of his resurrection:
Knowing this, that our old man is crucified
with him, that the body of sin might be
destroyed, that henceforth we should not serve
sin. For he that is dead is freed from sin.*

Stanley summarizes: "God wants the 'self' life
crucified. He does not want it dressed up, patched
up, under control, decorated, or ordained. He
wants it crucified."[5]

Gary Shores is an interesting case in point. His
wife, no longer willing to put up with his self-
centered approach to life, left him in January 1989
and divorced him six months later. For Gary, who
was saved at 12 and baptized at 18 years of age,
the divorce was more than traumatic. It was devas-
tating. As he recounts the story through his tears,
he says, "It broke me to my knees, and I've been on

---

5.   Stanley, *How to Handle Adversity,* 157.

my knees ever since." But he also acknowledges that "as stubborn as I was, that was the only way the Lord was going to get a hold of me."

In the time since the divorce became final, God has used Gary mightily to lead many young boys in his church to salvation: "God's hand has been in it all the way, in that He could use somebody as ignorant and stupid as I am to lead twenty-some young men to accept Christ as Savior." A man broken and crushed has experienced crucifixion of self and has yielded himself to God's will in his life. He says, "Trials and temptations only make us enjoy the joy and richness of life even more. Whatever comes out of this, I'll be satisfied, because all we can hope for is God's will in our lives. God will love me no matter how this thing turns out. The most important thing I have learned out of this is that we are like a child to a father. And when we humble ourselves as a child and go to the Father and ask his help, he'll help us no matter what we've done, no matter how bad things are."

Gary Shores went from a love for himself—"I was on a diet, committed more to losing weight than to God and to my marriage"—to a passion for young people. God had to allow Satan to destroy Gary's marriage in order to get his attention and to get him ready for heaven. Exceptional? No. Typical? Probably.

Since Christians are predestined for glorification (chapter one), it is only natural to assume that God would prepare them for the glorified existence. And, according to Paul, suffering is a part of the process: "For I reckon that the sufferings of this present time are not worthy to be compared with the glory which shall be revealed in us" (Rom. 8:18). Again, in 2 Corinthians 4:17-18, he indicates that afflictions are part of the preparatory process for the eternal state:

*For our light affliction, which is but for a moment, worketh for us a far more exceeding and eternal weight of glory; While we look not at the things which are seen, but at the things which are not seen: for the things which are seen are temporal; but the things which are not seen are eternal.*

Stanley claims that "Nothing compares with suffering when it comes to bringing God glory, for nothing else highlights our dependence, weakness, and insecurity like suffering."[6] He adds, "But suffering is also the way God brings honor and glory *to His children*...Adversity in this life, when handled properly, provides for the believer glory and honor *in the life to come*."[7] Adversity teaches the

---

6.　Stanley, *How to Handle Adversity*, 39.
7.　Ibid., 39-40 [emphasis added].

believer to yield to the lordship of Christ, thus preparing him for an eternity of surrendered service.

## A Loving Father and His Rebellious Children

Jesus said to pray, "Our Father." Gary Shores learned that "we are like a child to a father." The Apostle Paul was so impressed with the relationship that was his through salvation that he exultantly described believers as "sons of God" and "children of God" and used the endearing term "Abba Father" when speaking of God:

> *For as many as are led by the Spirit of God, they are the sons of God. For ye have not received the spirit of bondage again to fear; but ye have received the Spirit of adoption, whereby we cry, Abba Father. The Spirit itself beareth witness with our spirit, that we are the children of God: And if children, then heirs; heirs of God, and joint-heirs with Christ; if so be that we suffer with him, that we may be also glorified together.*

> Rom. 8:14-17

What a wonderful relationship the redeemed have with the Redeemer. His Father has become their Father. His inheritance has become their inheritance. His suffering has become their suffering. His glory has become their glory. But a relationship has two sides. The loving Father has done his part by making the relationship possible through the death and resurrection of his Son, Jesus Christ. He has not only offered salvation by grace, or unmerited favor, a gift, but he has also provided the faith necessary for his children to trust his Son: "For by grace are ye saved through faith; and *that* not of yourselves: it is the gift of God: Not of works, lest any man should boast (Eph. 2:8-9) [emphasis added]. Grace and faith are both gifts from the Father, and neither can be self-generated.

So what does he expect in return? He fully expects to be obeyed, just as any father does. John wrote that the identifying traits of believers are obedience and love (1 John 2:3-11). Jesus confirmed this by summarizing the hundreds of commandments in the Old Testament to just two in the New Testament, but the two are so comprehensive that they cover every aspect of man's relationship to God and to his fellow man:

> *Jesus said unto him, Thou shalt love the Lord thy God with all thy heart, and with all thy soul, and with all thy mind. This is the first and great commandment. And the second is like unto it, Thou shalt love thy neighbour as thyself.*
>
> Matt. 22:37-39

These are the boundaries inside which God expects his children to live and function while here on earth. Every parent sets boundaries for his children and anticipates that they will not cross those confines. When they do, the parent who truly loves his children is obliged to discipline them, not because he enjoys administering punishment, but because he knows his children must learn to live within the rules. If they do not learn it at an early age, they are sure to run afoul of the law and become burdens on society.

God is certainly no less a parent than any earthly mother or father. He is so loving that he has regenerated, indwelt, baptized, and sealed every believer with his own Holy Spirit. Not only is the Holy Spirit a Comforter (John 14:16, 26), but he is also an Interpreter of the prayers of the saints (Rom. 8:26-27). In his omniscience, God has provided everything that a Christian needs for life and death through his Son and his Spirit. For salvation, he requires only belief in his Son. Jesus said that "whosoever believeth" in the Son would have "everlasting life" (John 3:16). Paul and Silas told the Philippian jailer to "believe on the Lord Jesus Christ" for salvation (Acts 16:31). This establishes the Father-child relationship, and it is available only through the Son. But God is also interested in fellowship with his children, and that is only possible through a proper association with his Spirit.

What child has not known the experience of joyfully waiting for dad to come home from work?

When the child has "been good" all day, he cannot wait for dad to come driving up. He runs out to the car and gives dad a big hug. Not only is his relationship as a child secure, but his fellowship is solid and unbroken. The situation is entirely different, however, when the child has "been bad." Perhaps his mother has said, "You just wait till your dad gets home. You're going to get it then!" Suddenly, what is normally a very pleasant experience turns into a dreaded proposition. The child does not run out to the car and hug dad. He avoids him, and things just are not right until the fellowship is restored. The mother in this case is a type of the Holy Spirit in that she maintains the household and watches over the child in the father's absence. As the father's representative, she must be obeyed by the child.

A believer's fellowship with the Father depends on his obedience to the one who represents the Father, and that is the Holy Spirit. Believers are enjoined to "grieve not the Holy Spirit" (Eph. 4:30), "quench not the Spirit" (1 Thess. 5:19), "walk in the Spirit" (Gal. 5:16), and "be filled with the Spirit" (Eph. 5:18). Sin grieves the Holy Spirit. Rebellion against his promptings quenches the Spirit. Living according to our own will, in the flesh, means we are not walking in the Spirit. And refusal to confess sins and yield total control to God results in a state of not being filled with the Spirit. The relationship is secure, but the fellowship is broken. A little boy does not cease being a son just because he disobeys his mother, but he has no sweet communion with her or his father until the situation is corrected. He is still related but out of fellowship.

How is the situation corrected? The child may on occasion be restored through his own heartbroken confession and repentance. His tender heart may also be grieved by the ruptured fellowship, and he moves immediately to glue it back together. This is ideal. Every child—and every child of God—should be so sensitive to his father that he at once seeks reconciliation. It has been said of Charles Haddon Spurgeon that he often stopped walking down the street and offered a silent prayer because an evil thought had crossed his mind, and he wanted nothing to come between him and his Father. Every believer who has known the Spirit-filled life knows the pain and misery of being out of God's will and the joy of fellowship renewal.

But what of the child who does not instantly seek reconciliation? The caring parent knows that discipline is necessary in this case for the good of the child. Discipline reaffirms the proper relationship, restores the fellowship, and removes the burden of guilt. Again, our heavenly Father is much more a parent than any earthly mother or father could ever be, and he chastens, or disciplines, his children because he loves them and wants them to be partakers of his holiness, participants of his righteousness, and rejectors of mental attitude sins such as bitterness. The writer of the Book of Hebrews was very explicit about the relationship between love, discipline, and bitterness:

*And ye have forgotten the exhortation which speaketh unto you as unto children, My son, despise not thou the chastening of the Lord, nor faint when thou art rebuked of him: For whom the Lord loveth he chasteneth, and scourgeth every son he receiveth. If ye endure chastening, God dealeth with you as with sons; for what son is he whom the father chasteneth not? But if ye be without chastisement, whereof all are partakers, then are ye bastards, and not sons. Furthermore we have had fathers of our flesh which corrected us, and we gave them reverence: shall we not much rather be in subjection unto the Father of spirits, and live? For they verily for a few days chastened us after their own pleasure; but he for our profit, that we might be partakers of his holiness. Now no chastening for the present seemeth to be joyous, but grievous: nevertheless afterward it yieldeth the peaceable fruit of righteousness unto them which are exercised thereby. Wherefore lift up the hands of them which hang down, and the feeble knees; And make straight paths for your feet, lest that which is lame be turned out of the way; but let it rather be healed. Follow peace with all men, and holiness, without which no man shall see the Lord: Looking diligently lest any man fail of the grace of God; lest any root of bitterness springing up trouble you, and thereby many be defiled.*

Heb. 12:5-15

For the vast majority of children—and children of God—discipline of the father is sufficient, and fellowship is restored. Divine discipline is a sure sign of the Father's love for his children.

But what of the child who will not obey and who will not respond to discipline, who will not yield to the will of his parents, and has a rebellious nature? Most parents have likely had the experience of looking out the window and observing a child engaged in some forbidden activity such as fighting with a neighbor's child. One warning, and then two, and perhaps three, to "stop fighting" are followed by something similar to this: "If you don't stop fighting, you're going to have to come into the house." And if the parent looks out the window again and sees the child fighting, the ultimatum is issued, "Come on in this house right now!"

Are there sins for which a loving heavenly Father will call his children home? Scripture indicates that the believer can commit a "sin unto death," a sin for which he would suffer physical death and be called home (1 John 5:16):

*If any man see his brother sin a sin which is not unto death, he shall ask, and he shall give him life for them that sin not unto death. There is a sin unto death: I do not say that he shall pray for it.*

There are many examples in the Bible of those who were called home for committing a sin unto death. Moses, in a fit of anger, struck the rock that provided water for Israel in the wilderness[8] instead of speaking to it as God commanded, and was not allowed to go into the Promised Land. Aaron likewise was refused passage into the Promised Land because of this incident:

*And Moses lifted up his hand, and with his rod he smote the rock twice: and the water came out abundantly, and the congregation drank, and their beasts also. And the LORD spake unto Moses and Aaron, Because ye believed me not, to sanctify me in the eyes of the children of Israel, therefore ye shall not*

8.   The rock was a type of Christ (1 Cor. 10:4). Moses violated the type by striking it twice, when Christ was only to be smitten once.

*bring this congregation into the land which I
have given them.*

Num. 20:11-12

Ananias and Sapphira misrepresented themselves
to the church and were struck dead on the spot
(Acts 5:1-11). Paul wrote to the carnal Christians
at Corinth, who were guilty of gross violations of
the Lord's Supper, that many of their number had
died early: "For this cause many are weak and
sickly among you, and many sleep" (1 Cor. 11:30).

What is a sin unto death? The above examples
make it clear that it is no one specific sin, but it is a
sin that is so serious that it brings much disgrace
upon God, and he determines that normal discipline
is insufficient. In his exposition of 1 John 5:16, J. Vernon McGee has provided this excellent insight:

> Absalom also committed a sin unto death. I
> believe that Absalom was really a child of God,
> but he led a rebellion against his father, King
> David. I have observed something over a period
> of years. I have watched how God has dealt
> with troublemakers in the church. I've not only
> seen Him remove them by death, but I've also
> seen Him set them aside so that they were of no
> more use in the service of God at all. It is pos-
> sible to commit the sin unto death.[9]

9.    J. Vernon McGee, *Thru the Bible*, 5 vols. (Nashville:
Thomas Nelson Publishsers, 1983), 5:820.

Just as a loving earthly father or mother will call a child into the house when that child will not obey and will not yield to the will of the parent, so also a loving heavenly Father will call a believer home by physical death. Perhaps these are some of those who will be saved "as by fire" (1 Cor. 3:15) when they stand at the Judgment Seat of Christ and see all their works consumed as worthless in God's sight. McGee explains,

> I think that if a child of God goes on disgracing the Lord down here, the Lord will either set him aside or take him home by death. God doesn't mind doing that. I think he does it in many instances.[10]

Why must some of God's children experience the suffering that comes with the Refiner's fire? They must learn to yield to the sovereign lordship of Jesus Christ. They must learn to accept his will as readily on earth as it is accepted in heaven, even if it means they have to be crushed and broken. And, finally, they must learn that God intends to have fellowship with his children, and he will use discipline or death, if necessary, to have that fellowship. He is a loving Father who wants only what is best for his children. He is sovereign God who demands obedience. And our love and devotion to

---

10.  McGee, *Thru the Bible*, 5:820.

our Father ought to be such that we would sing
with the songwriter,

Take the dearest things to me, if that's how it
must be
To draw me closer to Thee;
Let the disappointments come, lonely days
without the sun,
If thro' sorrow more like You I'll become!
Take my houses and lands, change my
dreams and my plans,
For I'm placing my whole life in your hands;
And if You call me today to a land far away,
Lord, I'll go and Your will obey.
For whatever it takes to draw closer to You,
Lord,
That's what I'll be willing to do;
For whatever it takes to be more like You,
That's what I'll be willing to do
I'll trade sunshine for rain, comfort for pain,
That's what I'll be willing to do;
For whatever it takes for my will to break,
That's what I'll be willing to do.[11]

---

11. Lanny and Marietta Wolfe, "Whatever It Takes"
(Dimension Music, 1975). Distributed by The Benson
Company, 365 Great Circle Road, Nashville, Tennessee
37228.

# Chapter 3

# Tested in the Fire

Simon Peter, the apostle of hope to Israelites who had turned to Christ, addressed his first letter to the Christian Jews who were dispersed in Asia Minor. In the first five verses, he showed that believers are secure because they are elected by God the Father, sanctified by the Holy Spirit, redeemed by the blood of Jesus Christ, begotten by God the Father through the resurrection of Christ, and kept by the power of God through the Holy Spirit. To these believers who had lost everything for the cause of Christ, including their families, homes, and citizenship, these words must have been comforting and encouraging. The verses that follow, however, have sustained believers throughout the church age in times of crisis:

*Wherein ye greatly rejoice, though now for a season, if need be, ye are in heaviness through manifold temptations: that the trial of your faith, being much more precious than of gold that perisheth, though it be tried with fire, might be found unto praise and honour and glory at the appearing of Jesus Christ: Whom having not seen, ye love; in whom, though now ye see him not, yet believing, ye rejoice with joy unspeakable and full of glory: Receiving the end of your faith, even the salvation of your souls .*

1 Pet. 1:6-9

The context makes it clear that Peter was not talking about an inner struggle with evil when he spoke of temptations but was addressing undeserved suffering from without. These people were in the crucible of unwarranted misery for a "season," a short period of time when compared to eternity.

James, Paul, and the writer of Hebrews all talked about trials, troubles, testings, and suffering. Jesus himself said that his followers should not be dismayed by trials and unfair treatment at the hands of those who did not believe in him:

*These things have I spoken unto you, that ye should not be offended. They shall put you out of the synagogues: yea, the time cometh, that whosoever killeth you will think that he doeth God service. And these things will they do unto you, because they have not known the Father, nor me.*

John 16:1-3

Peter called it "the trial of your faith" (1 Pet. 1:7).

Why does faith have to be tested: Is not all faith the same? Could it be that some of the great "faith" proclaimers of the day, those who espouse health and wealth and who build great edifices for their own glory, do not have biblical faith at all? The Bible indicates that faith must be tested for purity, and true faith will be purified in the fiery trial.

**Faith Is Like Gold, But More Precious**

There are many elements that either look like gold or may be made to look like gold. Hundreds, perhaps thousands, of gold miners and traders have been financially devastated by so-called "fool's gold." When one takes a trinket, ring, or chain to a gold dealer today to be appraised, the dealer will first carefully look for approved markings indicating the purity under a magnifying glass. In the absence of such markings, he will apply some liquid substance to the article to determine if it really is gold or not. What appears to be gold may in fact be only gold-plated, gold-filled, gold brick, or have no trace of gold at all. Gold is a precious metal, the standard of the world's currencies, but it must be tested for purity.

The purest gold, of course, is that which contains the least amount of impurities. After gold is mined from the ground, it is placed in a red-hot furnace, or smelter, and heated until it melts. As J. Vernon McGee has observed, "The purpose is not to destroy the gold; it is to purify the gold. When the gold is melted, the dross is drawn off to get the pure gold."[1] For many years, McGee's "Thru the Bible" radio broadcast has begun with a wonderful old hymn, "How Firm a Foundation," in which the following verse is so appropriately found:

> When thro' fiery trials thy pathway shall lie,
> My grace, all sufficient, shall be thy supply;
> The flame shall not hurt thee; I only design
> Thy dross to consume, and thy gold to refine.[2]

Peter, then, compares the testing of gold by refining fire with the testing of faith by "the Refiner's fire." It is a beautiful comparison and particularly apt. And if gold, one of the most valued elements on earth, must be purified by being put in the fire until all the impurities are removed, why should anyone be surprised that something even more precious than gold should likewise be tested

1. McGee, *Thru the Bible*, 5:681.
2. Words, John Rippon's Selection of Hymns, 1787. *Baptist Hymnal* (Nashville: Convention Press, 1975), 383.

and purified? The true element known as gold is refined from the chunk that looks like gold but contains dross. The true element of faith is likewise refined from man's professed faith, which claims to be real faith but may be superficial. McGee explains God's refining process:

> When God tests us today, He puts us into the furnace. He doesn't do that to destroy us or to hurt or harm us. But He wants pure gold, and that is the way He will get it. Friend, that is what develops Christian character. At the time of *testing*, the dross is drawn off and the precious gold appears. That is God's method. That is God's school.[3]

The longer gold remains in the fire, the more impurities rise to the surface. As the impurities are removed, the gold becomes more and more pure, more and more precious, more and more valuable. Faith is like that. The more trials it goes through, the hotter the fire, the longer it is exposed to the fire, the more pure, precious, and valuable it becomes. W.T. Purkiser has observed that "It is when faith is 'tried by fire' that the dross of self-dependence and human reliance is burned away and the pure gold of trust remains."[4]

---

3.  McGee, *Thru the Bible*, 5:681.
4.  W.T. Purkiser, *When You Get to the End of Yourself* (Kansas City, Missouri: Beacon Hill Press, 1970), 34.

As precious as gold is, it is only a weak comparison to the faith of a saint of God or to "the precious blood of Christ" (1 Pet. 1:18-19) through which saints are redeemed. Peter said that the purest gold "perisheth" (1:7) and is "corruptible" (1:18). By implication, faith does not perish and the blood of Christ cannot be corrupted. Saints are dealing with things eternal, not temporal, and have the assurance of "an inheritance incorruptible, and undefiled, and that fadeth not away, reserved in heaven" (1:4).

A lovely thought must be made on this subject. It is said that the refiner knows the gold is pure when he looks into the liquid and sees his own face. Oh, the wonder of the very idea that God, the Refiner, looks into faith that is in the fire and is purified by the fire and sees himself! When the faith is pure, God sees his own image. And who is the expression, the image of god? It is Jesus Christ. When God peers into the purified faith of a believer, he sees his Son, the one in whose image believers are predestined to be conformed (Rom. 8:29). No wonder Paul could proclaim, "Christ liveth in me" (Gal. 2:20). Every believer should constantly ask himself the question, "Is my faith so pure that God himself sees Jesus when he looks on the inside of me?" Refined and purified faith reflects Jesus Christ.

## Untested Faith Is Suspect

The single greatest tragedy in ministry in recent years has been the proliferation of so-called faith preachers who have fooled a far too receptive and gullible radio and television audience into believing that faith is merely a function of the mind and that man's destiny is entirely dependent upon the amount of faith generated from within oneself. If a person wants to be healthy, all he has to do is believe he is healthy and command that fever, that sneeze, that cancer to leave his body. To be sick is to admit to little or no faith. If one wants to have lots of money, he merely exercises the faith to see himself as rich, rebukes the spirit of poverty, and calls the armored car to carry all his loot to the bank. To be poor is unthinkable among those with "overcoming faith."

These faith peddlers love to quote the last line of Isaiah 53:5, "by his stripes we are healed," in the first instance, ignoring the fact that the verse has to do not with physical but spiritual healing of "transgressions, iniquities, and the chastisement of our peace." The stripes and wounds inflicted upon Christ were for the healing of sin in mankind. Christ atoned for sin; redeemed mankind from the slavery of sin; provided reconciliation to God for man separated by sin; paid the death penalty for sin; satisfied, or propitiated, God the Father who was furious because of sin; and justified mankind so that God the Father could declare him righteous in spite of sin. To base a theology of physical healing on Isaiah 53:5 and the work of Christ on the cross is to exhibit gross ignorance and to diminish the purpose of his death. And to insist that one who has faith will never be sick is to ignore countless verses to the contrary and to deny that God may test faith through physical sickness or injury.

Faithmongers likewise use 3 John 1:2 as a proof text that God wants all his children to be rich, and all a child of God needs to be rich is faith: "Beloved, I wish above all things that thou mayest prosper and be in good health, even as thy soul prospereth." Who was the "beloved" that John was addressing? Was it the church? Was it those in the church who conjured up enough faith to believe it? Or was it "the well-beloved Gaius" to whom the letter was addressed in the first verse. The answer is obviously Gaius. John was wishing his friend prosperity and good health, not the entire church. Peter implied that believers may lose everything here on earth, as the Jews scattered in Palestine certainly had, but are not to evaluate their spirituality on earthly belongings. It is the heavenly inheritance (1 Pet. 1:4), the faith that stands the test of the fire (1:7), and the salvation of the soul (1:9) that matter.

This health and wealth doctrine is dangerous. David Wilkerson assesses the peril in this manner:

This perverted gospel seeks to make gods of people. They are told, "Your destiny is in the power of your mind. Whatever you can conceive is yours. Speak it into being. Create it by a positive mind set. Success, happiness, perfect health is all yours—if you will only use your mind creatively. Turn your dreams into reality by using mind power."

Let it be known once and for all, God will not abdicate His lordship to the power of our minds, negative or positive. We are to seek only the mind of Christ, and His mind is not materialistic; it is not focused on success or wealth. Christ's mind is focused only on the glory of God and obedience to His Word.

No other teaching so ignores the Cross and the corruption of the human mind. It bypasses the evil of our ruined Adam nature, and it takes the Christian's eye off Christ's gospel of eternal redemption and focuses it on earthly gain.

Saints of God, flee from this![5]

What happens when this type of faith is put to the test, as it inevitably must be? What is the result when the person who has been caught on the hook of

---

5. David Wilkerson, "A Prophecy Wall of Fire," quoted in *The Seduction of Christianity* (Eugene, Oregon: Harvest House Publishers, 1985), 21-22.

say-so faith suddenly becomes ill or has a financial reversal that lands him in the poorhouse? As he frantically adjusts the radio dial from one station to another seeking a faith "fix" to make everything all right, his "faith" flies out the window. Most tragically, however, his assurance of salvation flies out the same window, and he has absolutely nothing to fall back on but some con artist saying, "Just have faith, and everything will be wonderful."

Anybody can claim to have faith. Everybody can claim to have faith. But nobody can know he has faith until it has been tested. There are no shortcuts to maturity, either physical or spiritual. A baby boy cannot become a man without passing through the obstacle of adolescence, and a baby Christian cannot become an adult Christian without passing through a faith-challenging valley or two. John indicated as much in his distinctions between little children, young men, and fathers in the church:

*I write unto you, little children, because your sins are forgiven for his name's sake. I write unto you, fathers, because ye have known him that is from the beginning. I write unto you, young men, because ye have overcome the wicked one.*

1 John 2:12-13a

The little children knew Christ as Savior, having expressed the childlike faith needed for salvation.

The young men had been to battle with the devil and had overcome him in the strength of the Word of God (2:14). They had fighting faith. The fathers had a faith that recognized God as the source of everything, including their faith, a faith that trusted God completely in every situation. The faith of the fathers was such that they simply gave the battle to the Lord, knowing that he was all-sufficient, all-powerful, and able, as Paul told Timothy, "to keep that which I have committed unto him against that day" (2 Tim. 1:12).

The songwriter, Tracy Dartt, hit the nail square on the head in the second verse of "God on the Mountain":

> We talk of faith when we're up on the mountain,
> But the talk comes easy when life's at its best;
> It's down in the valley of trials and temptations,
> That's when faith is really put to the test.[6]

Untested faith is suspect. It may not be faith at all. It may simply disappear when the storms of life come. "All that glitters is not gold," and all that professes to be faith is not faith. H.N. Oswalt, whose story is told in chapter one, admits to "absolutely no fear" as he lay on the ground waiting

---

6.  Tracy Dartt, "God on the Mountain" (Gaviotta Music, 1976). Distributed by Kirk Talley Music, P.O. Box 1918, Morristown, Tennessee 37816.

for help. He likewise admits that he did not know if he had real faith until that moment when it was so severely tested. Now he knows. Kaye Bailey, the cancer victim of chapter two, struggled with cancer but not with her faith—it was unshakeable. It had been tested and found to be real.

John Sims is a chaplain in a Baptist hospital who lost a kidney to cancer at the age of 59. He admits he "wanted to die," but as a result of the test of his faith he has become far more sensitive to the needs of others, and has stopped being self-conscious and afraid of others. He has become one of the most respected counselors in Birmingham, Alabama. His empathy for others is obvious. What was it that made him a champion of Christian virtues? "I no longer have to be afraid of getting cancer, and you do," he says. "It's liberating to come that close to checking out and not checking out."[7]

If things could feel and express emotions, two of the most frightened items on earth would be a pine tree and a mobile home in a tornado or hurricane. Anyone who has ever viewed the damage from nature's fury in these two events can readily attest to the fact that pine trees and mobile homes usually suffer the brunt of the damage.

---

7. Address to cancer symposium held March 19, 1990, at Baptist Medical Center Princeton, Birmingham, Alabama. From personal notes of the author.

Pine trees often topple like dominoes, while the oaks continue to stand. What is the difference? Pines have a shallow root system, while the roots of the mighty oaks reach far into the earth. The oak has a grip on the earth that goes far beyond what the eye can see, and he refuses to loosen that grip when the winds howl around and through his branches. True faith is like that, "the substance of things hoped for, the evidence of things not seen" (Heb. 11:1). It is not the product of one's mind but is "the gift of God" (Eph. 2:8) and is rooted in him alone. When the gentle breezes have come, this faith in the one who is faithful has stood the test. When the thunderstorms of life have punished it, this faith has gripped the Lord a little tighter, and it has continued to stand and to extend its roots a little deeper. Finally, when a raging tornado or hurricane has come roaring around and through its limbs, it has held on for dear life to the One who has been faithful in all the smaller trials. Real faith is like an oak tree: it will be found to be deeply rooted when the tornadoes of life assault it.

False faith, on the other hand, is like the pine tree. It is rooted only in the mind of man. The roots are all near the surface. It can normally withstand the gentle breezes, but it starts to tremble in the thunderstorm and falls completely apart in the hurricane or tornado of life. Oh, it looked good growing up, rising much more quickly than the oak, boastfully pointing to itself as one that had a little something more than the other trees, but it was wrongly rooted to endure the test. And when it falls, as it surely will, it cannot be righted. So, too, the person who keeps the root structure of his faith near the surface and does not take a firm grip on the Lord Jesus Christ. When he falls in the maelstrom, it is often impossible to get him righted, because he has been deceived into trusting in himself, and his faith has no substance.

Buildings, too, are like faith. Some will withstand the storms, and some are even guaranteed hurricane or tornado proof. Oh, to have faith that is storm proof. But some buildings will not endure a severe storm. They look great when the sun is shining but fail when pelted by the wind and rain. If a building does not provide shelter in a storm, it is worthless. If faith does not withstand the storms of life, it is likewise worthless. Archer Thorpe has made this observation regarding buildings:

I was in Shreveport, Louisiana, for a week revival. I drove out to where a hurricane hit a community of homes. I saw many torn down, many in pieces. But I also saw many that were still standing without harm. Some had been built with flimsy and cheap material, while others were built with strength enough to withstand the storm. The storm revealed the character of the houses and of what material they were made. The purpose of Christ is not to eliminate the storms of life.

He came to give character. To His disciples, He said, "In the world ye shall have tribulation: but be of good cheer; I have overcome the world" (John 16:33b).[8]

Anybody can claim to have faith. Everybody can claim to have faith. But nobody can know he has faith until it has been tested.

## Purified Faith Brings Glory to God

Peter's understanding of faith refined in the fire has a radical twist. Not only does faith need testing to prove itself, but the testing brings glory to God:

*That the trial of your faith, being much more precious than of gold that perisheth, though it be tried with fire, might be found unto praise and honour and glory at the appearing of Jesus Christ.*

1 Pet. 1:7

In that same epistle, he added that regardless of the opinions of men, reproach for Christ's name glorifies him:

*If ye be reproached for the name of Christ, happy are ye; for the spirit of glory and of God*

---

8.  Message delivered October 26, 1983, at Loveless Park Baptist Church, Bessemer, Alabama. Notes of the Speaker.

*resteth upon you: on their part he is evil spoken of, but on your part he is glorified.*

1 Pet. 4:14

When a believer comes to understand that he is just an ambassador for Christ upon this earth, and that everything that he does or says reflects directly upon the one he represents, he can accept the fact that the testing of his faith and the resulting purified faith brings glory to God. The purification process, then, is for the spiritual profit of the believer and the glory of God.

Does God really receive glory through the trials, testing, and suffering of his children? He does. This glory comes because the Christian usually does not turn to the Lord for help in his daily walk until he encounters trouble. Oh, he should, but the sad fact is that he does not. The believer must recognize that the strength is not his, but the Lord's. The filling and power of the Holy Spirit are available only to the totally yielded and submissive believer. God understands human nature perfectly, and his ways are different than man's ways; therefore, he must let his children suffer at times to mold them in character and cause them to depend upon him. The one who trusts God implicitly in every situation likewise glorifies God in every victory.

The Lord told Paul, "My grace is sufficient for thee: for my strength is made perfect in weakness"

(2 Cor. 12:9). Paul countered with an understanding heart, "When I am weak, then am I strong" (2 Cor. 12:10).

Ignatius, martyred by Trajan, succumbed after saying, "Let the fire, the gallows, the wild beasts, the breaking of bones, the pulling asunder of members, the bruising of my whole body, and the torments of the devil itself come upon me, so that I may win Christ Jesus!"[9] In 1546, Michael Michelot went to his death after these words: "God has given me grace not to deny the truth, and will give me strength to endure the fire."[10] Suffering looks like weakness to the average man, but man's weakness can be strength in God. No one remembers those who hanged Ignatius or who burned Michael Michelot, but they are remembered over the centuries because they had a faith in a God that would sustain them through the experience of death and would deliver them safely on the other side. They had a faith that was greater than the gallows or the fire. They had a faith that counted it an honor to endure the ultimate test for Christ. They had a faith that was so pure it has glorified God for hundreds of years. They had a faith that agreed with the apostle when he wrote, "Wherefore let

9.   John Foxe, *Foxe's Book of Martyrs*, ed. Marie Gentert King (Old Tappan, New Jersey: Revell, 1981), 17.
10.  Ibid., 56.

them that suffer according to the will of God commit the keeping of their souls to him in well doing, as unto a faithful Creator" (1 Pet. 4:19). Why suffer? Simply to glorify God. Can any doubt that the purified faith of the martyrs glorified God?

With 1 Peter 4:19 as a backdrop, Helen Steiner Rice has written a beautiful and appropriate poem entitled, "Life's Bitterest Disappointments Are God's Sweetest Appointments,"[11] quoted below:

*Out of life's misery born of man's sins*
*A fuller, richer life begins,*
*For when we are helpless with no place to go*
*And our hearts are heavy and our spirits are*
*    low,*
*If we place, our poor, broken lives in GOD's*
*    HANDS*
*And surrender completely to HIS WILL and*
*    DEMANDS,*
*The "darkness lifts" and the "sun shines through"*
*And by HIS TOUCH we are "born anew"...*
*So praise GOD for trouble that "cuts like a*
*    knife"*
*And disappointments that shatter your life,*
*For with PATIENCE to WAIT and FAITH to*
*    ENDURE*

---

11.   Helen Steiner Rice, *Loving Promises Especially For You* (Carmel, New York: Fleming H. Revell Company, 1975), 47.

*Your life will be blessed and your future secure,*
*For GOD is but testing your FAITH and your*
    *LOVE*
*Before HE "APPOINTS YOU" to rise far above*
*All the small things that so sorely distress you,*
*For GOD'S only intention is to strengthen and*
    *bless you.*

And, one must quickly add, to glorify himself. God is glorified when his creatures recognize the omnipotence of the Creator and their own helplessness without him. He is glorified when his children yield to Solomon's challenge: "Trust in the LORD with all thine heart; and lean not unto thine own understanding. In all thy ways acknowledge him, and he shall direct thy paths" (Prov. 3:5-6). He is glorified when by faith his children trust him to do that which they could not possibly have done themselves. He is glorified when they say, "To God be the glory, great things he hath done."

Purified faith recognizes where the glory belongs. Purified faith brings glory to God. Barnhouse provides an excellent summary:

To the end God tells us to count it all joy when we fall into various kinds of testing (James 1:2). This is why the trial of our faith is much more precious than that of gold which perishes though it be tried in the fire (1 Pet. 1:7). We are being refined and purified. We are being tooled into the form that will glorify Him. We are confident that when the process is complete we shall come forth, made like the Lord Jesus Christ, and we shall be glad for every step of the way.[12]

And Purkiser adds,

That we do not enjoy the fiery trial goes without saying. What we need to remember is that even bitter medicine may be good for us. Those things in life which appear to us to be disappointments, obstacles, or hindrances may in fact be stepping-stones, not stumbling blocks.

Years ago Frances Ridley Havergal asked, "Did you ever hear of anyone being much used for Christ, who did not have some special waiting time, some complete upset of his or her plans first? I look at trial and training of every kind in this light—its gradual fitting of me to do the Master's work."[13]

Glory to God in the Master's work. That is the purpose of purified faith. Job said, "But he knoweth the way that I take: when he hath tried me, I shall come forth as gold" (Job 23:10). Praise the Lord for his refining fire. Praise the Lord for tested and purified faith.

---

12. Barnhouse, *Romans*, 4:85.
13. Purkiser, *When You Get to the End of Yourself*, 30.

# Chapter 4

# Believed by God's Children

There is a commercial for Northwest Airlines in which a harried executive responds to a number of demands by saying, "I can do that." After every demand that he appear in city after city on successive days, his answer is always, "I can do that." Finally, after reflecting for a moment, he asks, "How am I going to do that?"

Unfortunately, that seems to always have been the situation with the children of God. They always express confidence in themselves to run their lives, but then each of them misses the point entirely by asking, "How am I going to do that?" The truth is that most believers want to trust God up to a point but then insist on making it on their own. God wants to be believed by his children in everything for every step along life's pathway.

Enoch was one who so believed God with such a simple faith that the Bible records, "By faith Enoch was translated" (Heb. 11:5). How was he translated? By faith. Enoch was not said to be perfect, but he is one of two men—Noah was the other (Gen. 6:9)—who are said to have "walked with God" (Gen. 5:24), and God apparently enjoyed his company so much that he "took him" (5:24) without requiring him to go through death. Enoch is said to have had a testimony, which could only have come from God himself, "that he pleased God" (Heb. 11:5). And it was his faith that pleased God because, as the writer to the Hebrews quickly points out, "without faith it is impossible to please him" (11:6).

Enoch's walk with God must have been one of unbroken fellowship, for, as Amos observed, "How can two walk together except they be agreed?" (Amos 3:3). He must have been totally sold out to God, separated completely unto God, and unswerving in his perseverance, because he walked with the Lord for 300 years. What an epitaph! In a chapter (Genesis 5) where everyone else's tombstone recorded, "And he died," Enoch had no grave marker but had his life summarized in these four words: "Enoch walked with God."

Abraham was another fine example of one who believed God. Chosen through God's sovereignty in Ur of the Chaldees among idol worshippers, Abraham (then Abram) moved by faith "not knowing whither he went" (Heb. 11:8), trusted God for an heir, offered that heir as a sacrifice, and "looked for a city which hath foundations, whose builder and maker is God" (Heb. 11:10), all the while believing God. No wonder then that James, among others, records that "Abraham believed God, and it was imputed unto him for righteousness: and he was called the Friend of God" (James 2:23). His heirs did not do so well, however.

## The Children of Israel Wandered for Lack of Faith

There is perhaps no greater example of the absolute sovereignty of God than that of his dealings with the children of Israel. Of his own volition and in his own omniscience he chose them to be his people and cared for them, despite their rebellious natures and ungrateful attitudes.

A sovereign ruler is the final word, the power in his country. He is not to be questioned. The best example of sovereignty among mortals that I have ever witnessed occurred during a visit to the Neuschwanstein Castle in southern Germany.

Upon entering a certain room, many of us noticed that the ceiling was painted blue but with stars shining. Upon questioning as to why King Ludwig II would have a blue sky with stars in it on his ceiling, the guide replied simply, "A king is a king is a king." In other words, what the king wants, he gets, and what he orders happens.

It is no surprise, then, that the sovereign God of this universe could choose a people and could comfort his servant Moses with the seven "I wills" of redemption found in Exodus 6:6-8.

*Wherefore say unto the children of Israel, I am the LORD, and I will bring you out from under the burdens of the Egyptians, and I will rid you out of their bondage, and I will redeem you with a stretched out arm, and with great judgments: and I will take you to me for a people, and I will be to you a God: and ye shall know that I am the LORD your God, which bringeth you out from under the burdens of the Egyptians. And I will bring you in unto the land, concerning the which I did swear to give it to Abraham, to Isaac, and to Jacob; and I will give it you for an heritage: I am the LORD.*

Moses had, of course, just made the first demand upon Pharaoh that he let the children of Israel go to worship in the wilderness (Exod. 5:1).

Pharaoh had responded by increasing the workload by not providing straw for the bricks. Defeated and dejected, Moses questioned God's methods and intentions. After 400 years of slavery, the people were upset and at the point of despair. Yet it was at precisely this point that God reminded Moses that he, God, was still in charge, that he was YAHWEH, and that he remembered his covenant.

God kept his promises! He said in Exodus 19:4, "Ye have seen what I did unto the Egyptians, and how I bore you on eagles' wings, and brought you unto myself." In Exodus 20:2, he said, "I am the LORD thy God, which have brought thee out of the land of Egypt, out of the house of bondage." And in Joshua 1:2, God said, "Moses my servant is dead; now therefore arise, go over this Jordan, thou, and all this people, unto the land which I do give to them, even to the children of Israel."

By grace, God delivered and redeemed the children of Israel, brought them through the Red Sea, fed them manna, gave them sweet water, and delivered them from Amalek. They traveled to Mt. Sinai by the grace of God. Then God asked them if they wanted to receive and obey the law and commandments, and they said, "We can do that," or, "All that the LORD hath spoken we will do" (Exod. 19:8). At Mt. Sinai, God gave them a choice, grace or law. They forsook the free grace of God for the bondage of the law, trading eagles' wings for crutches, and man has limped along ever since that time asking the question, "How are we going to do that?" For 1500 years, from Sinai to Calvary, under ideal conditions, the children of Israel proved they could not keep the law or please God. What a contrast is presented in Exodus 19:18-24 where God, who had carried them on eagles' wings, warns them not to approach him at all lest they die:

> *And mount Sinai was altogether on a smoke, because the LORD descended upon it in fire: and the smoke thereof ascended as the smoke of a furnace, and the whole mount quaked greatly. And when the voice of the trumpet sounded long, and waxed louder and louder, Moses spake, and God answered him by a voice. And the LORD came down upon mount Sinai, on the top of the mount: and the LORD called Moses up to the top of the mount; and Moses went up. And the LORD said unto Moses, Go down, charge the people, lest they break through unto the LORD to gaze, and many of them perish. And let the priests also, which come near to the LORD, sanctify themselves, lest the LORD break forth upon them. And Moses said unto the LORD, The people cannot come up to mount Sinai: for thou chargedst us, saying, Set bounds about the mount, and sanctify it. And the LORD said unto him,*

*Away, get thee down, and thou shalt come up, thou, and Aaron with thee: but let not the priests and the people break through to come up unto the LORD, lest he break forth upon them.*

Oh, how sad to choose self-reliance over dependence on God. How sad that this sin always makes God unapproachable and fellowship with him impossible. How sad that this "way that seemeth right unto a man" should always prove in the end to be a path of "death" (Prov. 16:25).

The saddest episode, however, came at a place called Kadesh-barnea. It was from Kadesh-barnea that the spies were sent into the Promised Land, and it was to Kadesh-barnea that the majority of the spies brought their "evil report" of "giants" and "grasshoppers" instead of "milk and honey" (Num. 13:26-33). And it was at Kadesh-barnea that God sentenced an entire generation to death, with the exception of Joshua and Caleb, and turned Israel back into the wilderness for another 38 years (Num. 14:26-33). Israel had become addicted to self-effort, to saving herself. She no longer walked by faith, no longer trusted the God who had delivered her out of Egypt to deliver her into Canaan. She could not destroy God's purpose, but she did delay his blessing and did not enter the Promised Land. Through the eyes of the law, Israel saw giants so tall that God's eagles could not possibly overfly them. So she wandered.

## Christians Also Wander for Lack of Faith

God tested the faith of Israel at Kadesh-barnea. He wanted to be believed by his chosen people. He wanted to bless them. But their faith was not pure, so they buried their dead in the wilderness.

Unfortunately, there are giants in people's lives today that seem just as real as those giants in Canaan. They are giants that are seen through the eyes of unbelief, not the eyes of faith.

Unbelievers, by their very name and nature, cannot see past the giant of unbelief. The giants of rebellion, religion, and Satan loom large in their field of vision and obscure their view of the Savior, Jesus Christ.

Local churches and denominations may face such giants as bickering, lack of harmony, debt, lack of vision or direction, sin, apathy, and "We've never done it that way before." Many churches refuse to make any move by faith, demanding rather to see the end from the beginning and thus refusing to enter the Promised Land of God's blessings for them.

Individual Christians face countless giants in their lives. John warned of the daddy giant, "love of the world," and his three sons, "lust of the flesh, lust of the eyes, and the pride of life" in his first letter to the church:

*Love not the world, neither the things that are in the world. If any man love the world, the love of the Father is not in him. For all that is in the world, the lust of the flesh, and the lust of the eyes, and the pride of life, is not of the Father, but is of the world.*

1 John 2:15-16

Bad habits, debt, and unforgiveness are just a few of the many other giants Christians may face. And it is when faith in God is not exercised in the face of these giants that the child of God wanders in this Christian experience. No wonder our churches are not winning souls and are not growing in grace and knowledge. We've lost sight of the goal, the vision has been blocked, and we are wandering around in a stupor as individuals and churches because one or more giants is standing in the way.

What is the problem? Frankly, it is the same problem that plagued Israel, the problem of self-reliance. Far too many Christians, who by grace through faith have trusted God with their souls for eternity, absolutely refuse to trust him with their daily lives. Philip Yancey has appropriately written,

Could Jesus be repeating the biblical idea that man's self-sufficiency must be shattered—the same self-sufficiency which first reared its head in the Garden of Eden? Jesus reserved His strongest language to denounce the sins of pride and piousness. If self-sufficiency is the most fatal sin because it pulls us, as if by a magnet, from God, then indeed the suffering and the poor do have an advantage. Their dependence and lack of self-sufficiency are obvious to them every day. They must turn somewhere for strength, and sometimes that renewal is found in God. The enticing encumbrances of life—lust, pride, success, glamour—are too far from some to be striven for, and a tremendous roadblock to the kingdom is thus bulldozed.[1]

In the first chapter of Galatians, it is evident that the Judaizers had followed Paul into Galatia and told the people that in addition to trusting Christ they had to keep the Mosaic law or not be saved. This, of course, is pure heresy. It is adding to grace. It is doing rather than believing. It is faith plus something. It is the mark of every cult. It is perversion of the gospel.

Paul, who had started the church in Galatia, reacted with horror, prompted by the Holy Spirit. He called this teaching "another gospel," not "the gospel of Christ," and angrily declared that any preacher of such a heresy, man or angel, would be

---

1.　Yancey, *Where Is God When It Hurts*, 131.

"accursed" (Gal. 1:6-9). God will not tolerate mixing law with grace. The law was given to show man his helplessness to live up to God's standard. It is a mirror that reflects man's filthiness before God, but it does not wash him clean. It was not given to save, but to drive men to Christ for salvation. God has only one passing grade, and that is 100 percent. Nobody has ever passed, and nobody ever will, because nobody can.

And yet Christians keep trying to approach God on a daily basis by legalistic means, somehow believing that their acceptance is based on their performance. Despite Paul's wretched and futile attempts to live the Christian life without the power of the Holy Spirit in Romans seven, many think that salvation assures them of the ability to live the Christian life on their own. They do not understand that salvation by grace through faith must be followed by holy living by grace through faith. God knows we as believers cannot live the Christian life. He wants to live the Christian life through us. The Galatians were called to a life of grace, not works, and so are believers today.

Dr. Wayne Crumpton is a poignant example. The pastor of a relatively large Baptist church in Alabama, he recently lost his wife to cancer, the latest in a string of tragedies in his life. He and his wife lost one child at three years of age to a brain tumor, a son who had spent two years on a feeding tube and tracheotomy. Their first child had died after only 10 hours of life. His wife lost one child in miscarriage after six months. Dr. Crumpton says, "I thought we had paid our dues."[2]

But his wife got sick, and soon it was evident she was going to die. In the days preceding her death, Mrs. Crumpton proved to be "a great Christian. She handled it better than I did," he recalls. "She was a witness to the doctors and nurses."

And then, through his tears, Dr. Crumpton recounts his own journey through the valley:

I thought I could handle anything. Without her, I felt as helpless and hopeless as I could possibly feel. God's the only one that is there when everybody else is gone. He's the one you go to bed with. He's too loving to do anything spiteful or hurtful. He's too wise to do anything dumb. He does what's best for us. He's in control. We've got to be submissive to him.

He traveled the road God would have every believer travel, the road from self-reliance to helplessness and finally to total dependence on the God who not only saved him but also wanted to live the Christian life in him. It is rarely a pleasant road.

---

2.   Entire account is from an address to a cancer symposium at Baptist Medical Center Princeton, Birmingham, Alabama, on March 19, 1990. Notes of the author.

Yancey observes that "among the roll call of the victorious faithful in Hebrews 11 are those beaten to death, whipped, chained, stoned, and starved in the desert."[3] Many Christians cannot understand why God did not intervene more then and why he does not heal all Christians now.

We seem to reserve our shiniest merit badges for those who have been healed, featuring them in magazine articles and TV specials, with the frequent side-effect of causing un-healed ones to feel as though God has passed them by. We make faith not an attitude of trust in something unseen but a route to get something *seen*—something magical and stupendous, like a miracle or supernatural gift. Faith includes the supernatural, but it also includes daily, dependent trust in spite of results. True faith implies a belief without solid proof—the evidence of things not seen, the substance of things hoped for. God is not mere magic.[4]

God told Moses, "I will bring you in unto the land, concerning the which I did swear to give it to Abraham, to Isaac, and to Jacob" (Exod. 6:8a). This, of course, was not just any land but the land that God had promised, i.e., Canaan. God was

---

3. Yancey, *Where Is God When It Hurts,* 73.
4. Ibid.

again reminding Moses and the children of Israel that he remembered his covenant and that he was faithful to fulfill his promises. This was not some impotent, apologetic god saying he would try to get the children of Israel through the exercise of their free—and rebellious—wills to decide to go to Canaan. This was the omnipotent God promising he "will" bring them into the land of Canaan. Why? Because he "did swear to give it to Abraham, to Isaac, and to Jacob." He was the sovereign God who called Abraham, the miracle-working God who made possible the birth of Isaac, and the patient God who tolerated Jacob in his years of self-reliance.

God has a fascination, it seems, with the land of Canaan that exceeds the understanding of men. Perhaps it pertains to the birth of Christ, or the Temple, or the throne in Christ's millennial kingdom. Perhaps it has to do with the fact that he gave it to the patriarchs and the chosen nation Israel. Maybe it is all of these and more. Whatever the reason, he promised to bring the children of Israel "in unto the land."

Surely, God would have preferred to bring Israel into the Promised Land straightway. The land was theirs. He had given it to them. But because of unbelief, he had to bring them in through the wilderness and the death of a generation of unbelieving, though chosen, Israelites. J. Vernon McGee makes application of Canaan to the Christian life:

> The land is Canaan. It was promised by God to Abraham, Isaac, and Jacob. Canaan is *not* a picture of heaven. It is a picture of the Christian life as believers should be living it. Canaan typifies the heavenlies where we are blessed with all spiritual blessing—the believer has to walk worthy of his high calling for perfect enjoyment of spiritual blessing. This is done through the filling of the Spirit (Eph. 4:1-5:18). There is also warfare and battles to win. Believers sometimes live as if they are bankrupt in the wilderness of the world and never enter into the riches of His grace and mercy.[5]

Does this mean that God so wants to be believed and trusted by his children today and so wants them to walk in the Spirit and filled by the Spirit that he will do whatever is necessary to bring them out of the wilderness of unbelief and into the land of spiritual blessing? Yes, yes, a thousand times yes! God wants the best for his children, and the best is not the manna and quail of the wilderness but the milk and honey of the Spirit-filled life that is characterized by unshakeable faith in him. He will bring his children into right fellowship with

5. McGee, *Thru the Bible*, 1:220.

him one way or another, or, like the children of Israel who refused to walk by faith, he will take
them home. He wants what is best for his children,
and the best comes by trusting him.

## Justification Should Lead to Sanctification, A Holy Walk by Faith

The opposite of law for the Christian is not law-
lessness, but holy living under grace. Salvation by
grace is the necessary beginning, but holy living by
grace naturally follows.

As has been previously discussed, justification
is the act whereby God declares a believing sinner
righteous on the basis of the shed blood of Jesus
Christ. Man is accountable to God to be absolutely
perfect in mind, heart, and body, but no man is
capable on his own of such perfection. So God offers
a bookkeeping miracle to write off all man's sin and
declare him righteous as if he had never sinned at
all. God does this totally apart from anything in
man and wholly from his own heart and desire because he pleased to do it that way. Man is left to
take it or leave it. Man must admit he is a sinner
and look to Christ alone. He must also accept that
God declares him righteous in Christ. Otherwise,
he cannot be justified. Barnhouse simplifies:

If you want it in the simplest terms, it is this:
God wants you to believe His Word that He is
satisfied with the death of Jesus Christ instead of your death. The most important

thing that could ever be said about the death of Jesus Christ is that God the Father is satisfied with it. If He, the righteous judge, is pleased to remit all penalties against us by virtue of what the Saviour did in dying on the cross, then there is no case against us forevermore. That is the amazing thing about the faith that is set forth for us to believe. It is complete; it is eternal. It is merely a question of believing God's Word about a set of facts: the fact of our sin and the fact of the divine provision through the Lord Jesus Christ.[6]

God declares that men are lost sinners and then declares that believers are righteous in Christ. If one declaration is true because God said it, then the second is equally true because God said it, too. It is believing God that counts for righteousness, not works of the law. This is most clearly seen in the salvation of Abraham some 635 years *before* Moses was given the law at Mt. Sinai. And how was Abraham saved? "Abraham believed God, and it was counted unto him for righteousness" (Rom. 4:3). And what type of faith must a person have to be declared righteous? The Scripture is clear: "But to him that worketh not, but believeth on him that justifieth the ungodly, his faith is counted for righteousness" (Rom. 4:5).

---

6.   Barnhouse, *Romans*, 2:58.

As wonderful and necessary as justification is, however, it is not the end for the believer but the beginning of a whole new life. It is a life that is to be characterized by holiness, a life of sanctification. A believer cannot do as he pleases. A true child of God will not, indeed cannot, live in sin, because he has a new nature which is slave to Christ, not to sin.

It might be good at this point to make a clear distinction between justification and sanctification by comparing the two. Justification, for example, is an act, but sanctification is a process. Justification declares the sinner righteous, while sanctification makes him righteous. Justification is for a person, and sanctification is in a person. Justification removes the guilt and penalty of sin, but sanctification removes the growth and power of sin. Justification is not dependent on sanctification, but sanctification is dependent on justification, because justification is the foundation on which sanctification rests. Holy living, or sanctification, starts where justification ends; if holy living does not start, it is a good sign justification never happened. A person who has no desire to be holy has never been saved.

Positionally, then, believers are righteous in God's sight through justification. Conditionally, however, they may be something else altogether. Far too many believers are carnal, living in sin, and their growth is stunted. Neither physical birth nor spiritual birth makes a person grow, but it puts him in a position to grow. A baby that never grows is dead, and a person who claims to be born again but never grows erects a tombstone over his life as evidence he was stillborn. True believers cannot continue to live in sin. The very thought horrified the Apostle Paul: "What shall we say then? Shall we continue in sin, that grace may abound? God forbid. How shall we that are dead to sin, live any longer therein?" (Rom. 6:1-2)

What a ghastly thought! Can a believer who by position is sure for heaven live in a condition of sin? By no means. The doctrines of salvation by grace through faith and eternal security of the believer by God's declaration are too easily misunderstood. A Christian's condition ought to match his position. Believers are not saved by leading holy lives—that adds works to grace—but lead holy lives because they are saved. In no way is the overflowing, overwhelming, incomprehensible abundance of grace designed to encourage sin. It discourages sin.

What was it that so distressed Jesus in the garden (Mark 14:32-34) to the point that he likely would have died right there if an angel had not strengthened him (Luke 22:41-44)? Was it the prospect of physical death? Of course not. That was the reason he came to earth. That was his mission.

Was it not the fact that sin would break the fellowship he had known with the Father from eternity past? He who knew no sin was about to be made sin, and he knew his Father so abhorred sin that he would turn his back and withdraw himself, and their sweet communion would be broken for the only time in eternity. He was about to suffer not only physical death on the cross of Calvary, but also spiritual death, or separation from God. Did Christ not cry out in horror, "My God, my God, why hast thou forsaken me" (Matt. 27:46)? Was Christ sanctified? Of course he was. Set apart for God, the holiest person who ever lived, and yet he recognized that sin would close the door between him and his Father.

Sanctification is horrified at sin. Why? Because, like Christ, it is terrified at the prospect of anything interfering with the fellowship that the sanctified one has known with the Father. Why live holy lives? For the sake of the fellowship and for the sake of Christ: "For he hath made him to be sin for us, who knew no sin; that we might be made the righteousness of God in him" (2 Cor. 5:21).

Paul pleaded with believers to consecrate, or set apart as holy, their bodies for Christian service:

*I beseech you therefore, brethren, by the mercies of God, that ye present your bodies a living sacrifice, holy, acceptable unto God, which is your reasonable service. And be not conformed to this world: but be ye transformed by the renewing of your mind, that ye may prove what is that good, and acceptable, and perfect, will of God.*

Rom. 12:1-2

Why present the body and not the soul or mind or spirit? The body is the means by which people express themselves; thus, Paul certainly means the total being, the personality. The mind, the will, the affections, and the Holy Spirit can all use the body. In other writings, Paul pointed out that the body is the temple of the Holy Spirit (1 Cor. 6:19-20), Christ is to be magnified in the body (Phil. 1:20), and the life of Jesus is to be made manifest in the body (2 Cor. 4:10). Given his mercy, his indwelling, his eternal life, and his commission to ambassadorship, a rational decision by the believer should be to yield to Christ. Paul called this a "reasonable service" or a spiritual ministry. It just makes good sense. It is reasonable.

Sanctification implies not being "conformed to this world." One who looks, acts, smells, and sounds like unbelievers is conformed to this world. One who lives like the world on the job, at school, or at home is conformed to this world. One who shines his halo for Sunday services but spews out the meanest and dirtiest gossip imaginable through the week is a hypocrite, an actor, and is conformed to this world.

The believer is not to be conformed but "transformed" (Rom. 12:2). "It is the word *metamorphoomai* which has given us our word metamorphosis. When a tadpole is changed into a frog or when a grub becomes a butterfly, we speak of it as metamorphosis."[7] It is the word translated "transfigured" when speaking of Christ in Matthew 17:2. What happened to Christ on the Mount of Transfiguration? His glory, the shekinah glory of God, which was on the inside of him, was revealed on the outside. The tadpole is a frog waiting to be revealed. The caterpillar is a butterfly waiting to be revealed. Jesus, the eternal beloved Son of God, "took upon him the form of a servant" (Phil. 2:7), and for a moment unveiled himself to manifest the glory that was his "before the world was" (John 17:5) and with which he will come again (Rev. 19:11-16).

A frog will never again be a tadpole. A butterfly will never again be a caterpillar. Christ will never again be a servant. And Christians will never again be lost sinners, so Paul says we are to quit acting like we are lost and start living like the new creations we have now become. It is possible for Christians with the new nature to live a transformed life. If we do

7.    Barnhouse, *Romans,* 4:27.

not, it is because we have not made use of the power that is within us since we accepted Christ as our Savior and were indwelt by the Holy Spirit. This new way of thinking, or transformation of the mind, brings believers to approve (prove by testing) and desire God's will in our lives. Then we find that God's will is good for us. What a shame that God had to send a messenger to beg his children to yield to him and walk in holiness that the beauty of the inside might be revealed on the outside. Butterfly believers, not caterpillar Christians, are what God expects and the world needs.

Peter's discussion of the trial of faith was immediately followed by an exhortation to holiness:

*Wherefore gird up the loins of your mind, be sober, and hope to the end for the grace that is to be brought unto you at the revelation of Jesus Christ; as obedient children, not fashioning yourselves according to the former lusts in your ignorance: but as he which hath called you is holy, so be ye holy in all manner of conversation; because it is written, Be ye holy; for I am holy.*

1 Pet. 1:13-16

As obedient children, believers ought to expect to live holy lives. It is rightly demanded by a holy God, who is the standard, the model. True devotion to God, Peter implies, expresses itself in holy speech and conduct. Holiness is as accurate an indicator of the spiritual life as our vital signs are to our physical lives. It is to this holy, sanctified, Christlike image that we as believers are predestined (Rom. 8:29). It is to be achieved by faith, as we trust Christ every single day to lead us "in the paths of righteousness for his name's sake" (Ps. 23:3). God wants to be believed by his own children.

# Chapter 5

# Teaching Love Through Trials

It is amazing to witness the consistency with which those who have experienced great trials testify to discovery of a love for God and a joy they never knew before. There is something about the trial that causes the believer to come to terms with God's love for him in a way that is seemingly not possible to grasp any other way.

Lazelle Edwards knew the fear of cancer.[1] She lived from one examination to the next, dreading a recurrence of the disease that caused her to lose a

---

1. For Lazelle Edwards' complete testimony, see appendix.

breast in a radical mastectomy. She realized anger at God and the frustration of trying to find his will for her life while dealing with cancer at the same time. In the aftermath of surgery, she recalled: "I felt God's wonderful love, care, protection, and peace. I felt He had dropped a veil around me. I was His, and nothing could harm me, not even Satan." The experience was such, she said, that "sometimes I felt I was in the realm of heaven." The ladies in her Sunday School class "reacted in horror" when she told them she was glad for the illness because of her new closeness with Christ.

And what was her opinion of the God who put her through the trial? She answers, "Oh, if every person could know this Lord as I now know Him! I want to praise Him always. I am satisfied with a peace, joy, and love of God beyond all I'd ever dreamed."

## Peter Learned Real Love Through Trials

Throughout recorded history, God has asked people questions, not just idle questions but deep, penetrating, searching inquiries that go to the very hearts of the people. In the Old Testament, for example, God asked Adam, "Where art thou?" (Gen. 3:9). He asked Abraham, "Is anything too hard for the LORD?" (Gen. 18:14). Jacob was required to answer the question, "What is thy name?" (Gen. 32:27). In Exodus 4:2, God asked Moses, "What is that in thine hand?" God asked the prophet Jeremiah, "Is there anything too hard for me?" (Jer. 32:27)

Jesus Christ continued putting people on the spot in the New Testament by asking tremendous questions. To blind Bartimaeus he queried, "What wilt thou that I should do unto thee?" (Mark 10:51), or "What do you want me to do, Bartimaeus?" Concerning the resurrection, Jesus asked Martha, "Believest thou this?" (John 11:26). He asked Martha's sister Mary a question regarding Lazarus in John 11:34, "Where have ye laid him?" In Matthew 16:13, he asked the disciples, "Whom do men say that I the Son of man am?" Two verses later, he required them to deal with their own understanding of his deity by inquiring, "Whom say ye that I am?"

The ultimate question, however, was asked of Peter as Jesus commissioned him to be an apostle. Jesus asked simply, "Lovest thou me?" (John 21:15, 16, 17)

Peter had a desperate need to be reinstated. When Jesus had told the disciples that they would not stand by him, Peter proudly proclaimed he would never deny Christ: "Though all men shall be offended because of thee, yet will I not be offended" (Matt. 26:33). John records that Peter asserted, "I will lay down my life for thy sake" (John 13:37). Yet as Jesus stood before the high priest, Peter's backbone turned to jelly, and he vehemently denied being a disciple of the Lord three times (John 18:15-27).

In response to Peter's threefold denial, Jesus gave him a threefold commission. In John 21:15, Jesus told this disciple who not many days afterward would deliver the great sermon on the Day of Pentecost, "Feed my lambs." Every adult, and particularly every pastor, in a church ought to tend the little ones. If young people in the church do not do right, maybe it is because the adults did not teach them right. When a church has to constantly beg for youth and children workers, it is begging for problems in the future. Peter was first admonished to take care of the youngest, most immature, most helpless members of the flock. His second commission from the Lord was to "feed my sheep" (John 21:16). In other words, Jesus was saying, "Take care of my sheep, shepherd them, herd them, lead them to pasture." Finally, in verse seventeen, Jesus uses the same verb he used in verse fifteen, telling Peter to "feed my sheep,"[2] an indication that all the flock needs spiritual food, the little ones and the old ones alike.

Preceding each of the three commissions, however, was a question, translated into English as,

2.  *The Zondervan Parallel New Testament in Greek and English,* 340-341.

"Lovest thou me?" He did not ask Peter, nor has he ever asked his disciples:

1. "Do you love the church?"
2. "Do you love the denomination?"
3. "Do you love discipleship training?"
4. "Do you love Sunday School?"
5. "Do you love the choir?"
6. "Do you love doctrine?"
7. "Do you love serving me?"

Jesus simply asked, "Do you love me?"

The English translation does not do justice to the depth of meaning of the wordplay that took place that day between Jesus and Peter. Peter twice failed to answer the Lord's question. It has been widely and well documented in countless dictionaries, commentaries, and reference Bibles that Jesus in verses fifteen and sixteen used the verb agapas ("deeply love; used of divine love...and of the love which the law demands...")[3], while Peter answered with the verb *phileo* ("am fond of. It is a lesser degree of love than *agapas*")[4]. In verse seventeen, Jesus uses Peter's word, *phileis*.[5] Ed Wheat

---

3. *The Holy Bible*, Scofield Reference ed. (New York: Oxford University Press, 1945), 1145-1146.
4. Ibid., 1146.
5. Ibid.

has made the following observations concerning *agape*:

1. *Agape* love means action, not just a benign attitude.
2. *Agape* love means involvement, not a comfortable detachment from the needs of others.
3. *Agape* love means unconditionally loving the unlovable, the undeserving, and the unresponsive.
4. *Agape* love means permanent commitment to the object of one's love.
5. *Agape* love means constructive, purposeful giving based not on blind sentimentality but on knowledge: the knowledge of what is best for the beloved.
6. *Agape* love means consistency of behavior showing an ever-present concern for the beloved's highest good.
7. *Agape* love is the chief means and the best way of blessing your partner and your marriage.[6]

The important thing to note is that Peter would not lie to Christ and could not bring himself to say that he loved the Lord with *agape*, or divine, love. He could only say that he loved the Lord with *phileo*, or brotherly, love. Peter was grieved that the Lord knew his heart and knew that his love

---

6. Ed Wheat, *Love Life For Every Married Couple* (Grand Rapids: Zondervan Publishing House, 1980), 120.

had not yet reached the *agape* level. What a poignant moment that must have been. Not to be deterred, however, Jesus proceeded to tell Peter that he, too, would be crucified (21:18) and then said to Peter, "Follow me" (21:19). In other words, Jesus said, "Peter, are you *now* willing to die for me?"

With all his heart, Peter surely wanted to tell his Messiah that he truly loved him with a divine love, yet with all his heart he knew he could not. But that is not the end of the story. Some thirty years later, as Peter writes his first epistle to the dispersed Jews in Asia Minor, he has discovered *agape* love, for that is the very word he uses in 1 Peter 1:8, "Whom having not seen, ye *love*; in whom, though now ye see him not, yet believing, ye rejoice with joy unspeakable and full of glory" [emphasis added]. What has happened to this man who knew Christ intimately, yet could profess no more than a brotherly love for him, that would cause him to say to those who never saw Christ, "You truly love him," and, by implication, "I truly love him, too"?

Yes, he has seen the resurrected Christ. Yes, he has witnessed the ascension. Yes, he has been selected by God and empowered by the Holy Spirit to preach the Pentecost sermon, seeing 3000 souls saved at one time. Yes, he has been selected to take the gospel of Jesus Christ to the Gentile centurion,

Cornelius. Yes, he has seen the sick healed, the dead raised, multitudes won to Christ. And, yes, he has seen prison doors shaken. He has, in a word, witnessed the mighty power and love of the Lord God in his life. But these things have only reinforced God's love for him, and, while they certainly contributed to his love for God, they did not by themselves bring him to love the Lord with all his heart.

No, there was something more. Peter learned real love for Christ through trials. He was jailed, threatened, beaten, and told not to preach the gospel of Jesus Christ. He was placed on Herod's death row, only to be delivered by an angel. Christ himself had told Peter he would die by crucifixion. Oh, he had known the might power of the Holy Spirit in his life since Christ had returned to the right hand of the Father, but he had also known heartache, pain, and sorrow. He had certainly grieved at the sin and death of Ananias and Sapphira, the death of Stephen, and the execution of James. He had surely been embarrassed by the public rebuke of Paul (Gal. 2:11-14), his junior in the ministry. But it was in these trials that Peter, who had once rebuked the Lord for mentioning his upcoming death (Matt. 16:22), took up his own "cross" and followed Christ. It was in these trials that Peter really came to understand his Lord and to love him. And it was here that a rugged old fisherman could so preach the love of Jesus that he knew the readers of his letter, who had not seen Jesus, had yet given to Jesus the love of their hearts. Peter, who along with James and John had witnessed the transfiguration of Christ, had himself been transformed into an apostle of love.

## Testing Brings Joy

Paul wrote to the church at Galatia: "But the fruit of the Spirit is love, joy, peace, longsuffering, gentleness, goodness, faith, meekness, temperance: against such there is no law" (Gal. 5:22-23). It is interesting that, while all of these are considered the fruit, not fruits, of the Spirit, they are nevertheless given in an order that the Holy Spirit thought important. And second to love is joy, a virtue too often lacking in the lives of most Christians. Chuck Swindoll has written this concerning joy:

There seems to be more of everything these days than joy. There's certainly more Bible study than joy. There is more prayer than joy—more church attendance, more evangelism, more activity, even more discernment than joy. And those of us who are leaders in religious service are often a major cause.

Some Christians look like they've been baptized in lemon juice. Many have such long faces they could eat corn out of a Coke bottle!

There are some exceptions, but therein lies the problem. Why are the joyful ones the exceptions?

If I read the Book correctly, joy is the runner-up virtue. If the "fruit of the spirit" is listed in the order of importance, love gets the blue ribbon, joy the red, right? If God awarded us medals, as they do in the Olympics, love would win the gold, joy the silver, and peace the bronze. I call that second-place finisher significant! Where are all the silver-medal eagles? We need more![7]

In the first chapter of 1 Peter, the apostle not only testified to the divine love that he and his readers had come to know but also of the joy they shared because of the trials they endured. In verse six, he proposed that they had joy in present sufferings: "Wherein ye *greatly rejoice*, though now for a season, if need be, ye are in heaviness through manifold temptations" [emphasis added]. What a radical idea! Christians not only find joy in suffering, but they "greatly rejoice." Surely this is a supernatural imparting of the fruit of the Spirit called "joy." The implication is that when we as believers understand that trials are for God's glory and our spiritual profit, we can delight in being

7.   Charles R. Swindoll, *Living Above the Level of Mediocrity* (Waco: Word Books, 1987), 193.

grieved. And the record of the martyrs is that they counted it a privilege to be considered worthy of dying for Christ.

This phenomenon is not limited to the spiritual arena, although it is much more common there. The kamakazi pilots of World War II willingly died for Japan, because they believed they would gain "heaven" by their self sacrifice. Moslem terrorists today believe the same thing. This, in a way, is spiritual, though misguided and not of the Holy Spirit. In a truly secular setting, the example of Jeremiah Denton needs to be told. After seven and one-half years of captivity in North Vietnam, Denton, a Navy captain, was released along with the other captives and flown to Clark Air Base in the Philippines. As the senior officer aboard the C-141 aircraft, he was expected to make a few brief remarks upon arrival. No one ever expressed love for his country more than did Denton, when he declared for all the world to hear, "We are honored to have had the opportunity to serve our country under difficult circumstances. We are profoundly grateful to our Commander-in-Chief and to our nation for this day. God bless America."[8] If people can rejoice in suffering for love of a country, a love which cannot compare to the divine love of which

---

8. Jeremiah A. Denton, Jr., *When Hell Was In Session* (Mobile, Alabama: Traditional Press, 1982), 178-179.

Peter speaks, why should it seem strange that Christians would rejoice in present sufferings for love of Christ?

It is not just the present sufferings which bring joy to believers, however, but also joy in a personal Savior. The love that Peter spoke of in 1 Peter 1:8 was in a Savior made real to believers by the Holy Spirit and in whom they had an active confidence by faith. Peter, perhaps knowing that no human word could ever describe it, called it "joy unspeakable and full of glory." It was so great it could not be expressed, but he knew he had it, and he knew it filled him with heaven's glory while he was yet on earth. Someone has said, "I'm drinking from my saucer, 'cause my cup's overflowed." That must have been the sensation Peter experienced as he contemplated what his personal Savior had done for him and what he was going to do as Peter's faith ended in sight. Peter and his readers had been saved from the penalty of sin and the power of sin, but one day they would be saved from the very presence of sin, receiving the final "salvation" of their souls (1:9). What joy!

Testing not only brings joy in present suffering and in a personal Savior but also in prophesied salvation. As Peter went on to explain in verses 10-12, salvation through Christ was the theme of Old Testament prophecy and of New Testament preaching. The Messiah had to suffer, because suffering was the door of entrance into his glory. As a result of his suffering, grace could and would be extended to all who would believe, Jew and Gentile alike. The Old Testament prophets, writing by the "Spirit of Christ" (1:11), though maybe not fully understanding why Messiah must suffer, nevertheless wrote of his sufferings "and the glory that should follow." Salvation is likewise the theme of New Testament preaching "by them that have preached the gospel" (1:12). New Testament apostles proclaimed, and gospel preachers today still shout the good news that because Christ suffered salvation is offered, and their message is from the same Holy Spirit that inspired the Old Testament prophets. Can anyone honestly doubt the veracity of the Bible, that "all scripture is given by inspiration of God" (2 Tim. 3:16), or that there is a Spirit-inspired unity in Old Testament prophecy and New Testament preaching when he reads these verses? Even angels take an intense interest in what God is doing on earth for the salvation of mankind, according to verse twelve. How amazing it must be to them that God would not only agree to save such sinful creatures but would also do it through the suffering and death of his only begotten Son. It is through testing and trials that the believer truly comes to rejoice "with joy unspeakable and full of glory," in a salvation so amazing that it is the wonder of the universe. Joy in a personal Savior and prophesied salvation alone is wonderful, but is superficial by comparison to that joy that comes through present suffering. God multiplies joy through testing.

What was it that Lazelle Edwards said about the joy that comes after the testing? "Oh, if every person could know this Lord as I know Him! I want to praise Him always. I am satisfied with a peace, a *joy*, and love of God beyond all I'd ever dreamed."[9] Testing brings joy.

## Enduring Testing Brings Rewards

After Abram had armed 318 of his servants and rescued his nephew Lot from the kings of the East, he was blessed and encouraged in the faith by the king of Salem, a mystery man named Melchizedek. But Abram was also met by the king of Sodom, who tempted Abram by offering him all the wealth he had captured from the kings of the East. In a tremendous act of faith, Abram refused the king's booty because it had deadly strings attached. In Genesis 7:1, the LORD appeared to Abram and reminded him that he, the LORD, was Abram's shield, or protection from all danger, and his "exceeding great reward." Abram had done well to

9. Lazelle Edwards' complete testimony is printed in appendix. Quote from testimony [emphasis added].

refuse Sodom's treasure because God would indeed prosper him and would be all the reward he needed.

In the fifth chapter of Romans, Paul wrote that there are rewards associated with the endurance of testing. Some of God's most precious gifts are accumulated as a result of tribulations: "And not only so, but we glory in tribulations also: knowing that tribulation worketh patience; and patience, experience; and experience, hope" (Rom. 5:3-4). Tribulations are common to all humanity, but only the Christian can triumph over them in absolute glory. A human leaves the safety of the mother's womb to be born under great pressure and a gasping struggle for life. He gradually learns to care for himself and sees much suffering before coming to his own deathbed. Man is born to these troubles, but a true Christian glories in them.

"Tribulation" comes from the Latin verb, *tribulare*, meaning "to press, to oppress, to afflict."[10] The Greek word used in the New Testament is "thlipsis, and originally conveyed the idea of 'pressing together, pressure.' "[11] The idea is that of grapes or olives being pressed in a vat with such crushing pressure that the juice or oil would be squeezed out. Barnhouse has said that "Christians

---

10.  Barnhouse, *Romans*, 2:73.
11.  Ibid.

were the first to think of themselves as being in the vat like grapes or olives, and being pressed to the point where their joy ran out like wine or oil."[12] It is only in crushing pressure, tribulations, and infirmities that believers realize God's power to distill glory and joy from pain.

It is doubtful if anyone has ever testified, "It was on the mountaintop when the sun was shining bright and everything was going just right that I learned patience, experience, and hope." On the contrary, it is in the vat of great pressure that these lessons are learned and these rewards attained. A dear lady in North Carolina once asked the Lord to give her patience, and the Lord gave her five children to care for almost immediately. How ironic that God, in order to give her patience, gave her something to sorely try her patience. Is that not what the apostle Paul said in Romans 5:3—"knowing that tribulation worketh patience"? In other words, the steadfastness and endurance which characterizes patience has its very source in tribulation. If there is no suffering, patience is not tested, strengthened, or allowed to reach full strength and maturity. Patience itself is a reward of enduring testing.

But there is also a reward that springs from patience itself. Job, perhaps the most sorely tested

---

12.   Barnhouse, *Romans*, 2:73.

and patient man who ever lived, was blessed not only spiritually but materially by the Lord for his faithfulness and patience: "And the LORD turned the captivity of Job, when he prayed for his friends: also the LORD gave Job twice as much as he had before" (Job 42:10). "So the LORD blessed the latter end of Job more than his beginning" (42:12). Paul, however, was not talking about material blessings in the fifth chapter of Romans. He said that the source of experience is patience, which comes from tribulation. The word, "experience," in the King James Version is translated "character" in the New International Version.[13] In his exposition of Romans 5:4, Everett F. Harrison has written,

> The value of perseverance is that it develops "character." Job sensed its worth, saying in the midst of his troubles, "When he has tried me, I shall come forth as gold" (Job 23:10, RSV). The word rendered "character" indicates tested value. The newborn child of God is precious in his sight, but the tested and proven saint means even more to him because such a one is a living demonstration of the character-developing power of the gospel. When we stand in the presence of God, all

13. *The Zondervan Parallel New Testament in Greek and English* (Grand Rapids: Zondervan Bible Publishers, 1975), 454.

material possessions will have been left behind, but all that we have gained by way of spiritual advance will be retained. This progress is a testimony to God, so it rightly has a place in glory.[14]

The reward then of patience is proven or tested value and character that can be gained in no other way than through endurance of trials. Endurance develops proof of a person's Christianity and of Christ's power. Paul told young Timothy that "all that live godly in Christ Jesus shall suffer persecution" (2 Tim. 3:12), but God likewise promised that "they that wait upon the LORD shall renew their strength; they shall mount up with wings as eagles; they shall run and not be weary; and they shall walk, and not faint" (Isa. 40:31).

Experience, or character, is said by Paul to produce "hope" (Rom. 5:4), another of the by-products or rewards of enduring testing. Without Christ, the unbeliever has no hope whatsoever, but the believer has a confident expectation in salvation from the penalty of sin, the power of sin, and ultimately, the presence of sin. The believer does not just have the hope of salvation, however, but also the "hope of the glory of God" (Rom. 5:2). This,

---

14. Everett F. Harrison, "Romans," in *The Expositor's Bible Commentary*, ed. Frank E. Gaebelein (Grand Rapids: Zondervan Publishing House, 1976), 10:57.

according to Barnhouse, "is nothing less than that he shall actually possess that glory of God, in an eternally growing degree." He continues, "We shall be like the Lord and shall manifest His glory. It is the closest possible union with God and His glory."[15] The true hope of the Christian, then, is that he will possess the glory of God with perfect knowledge, purity, and love. This hope is the consummation of a series of rewards for those who have been justified and have been subjected to tribulations. "By the tutelage of suffering," Harrison asserts, "the Lord is fitting us for his eternal fellowship."[16] Oh, to know and have his glory!

Real love, real joy, real rewards. These are just some of the wonderful gifts God gives his children in real trials.

---

15. Barnhouse, *Romans*, 2:101.
16. Harrison, "Romans," *Expositor's*, 10:57.

# Chapter 6

# Suffering Identified with the Believer

The New Testament beautifully pictures the church as the body of Christ and the future bride of Christ. Christ is identified as "the head of the church" (Eph. 5:23) in the great instructional passage on the married life of Spirit-filled believers as compared to Christ and his church (Eph. 5:21-33). But what does it mean to be the body of Christ? Is the relationship between Christ and his church really as close and as intimate as that of the head and the body in a human being?

---

Jesus described the intimacy between himself and his followers as that of a vine and branches. He said, "I am the vine, ye are the branches: He that abideth in me, and I in him, the same bringeth forth much fruit: for without me ye can do nothing" (John 15:5). Just as the body cannot survive, function, or produce outside the head, so the branch is useless and dead outside the vine. Jesus said as much in verse four of the same chapter: "Abide in me, and I in you. As the branch cannot bear fruit of itself, except it abide in the vine; no more can ye, except ye abide in me." Just as the physical head and body know each other intimately, so the spiritual must also become intimate.

## Suffering Is a Requirement to Really Know Christ

In his great prison epistle to the church at Philippi, the Apostle Paul bared his soul concerning the Christian experience and the working of the mind, life, and nature of Christ in every believer generally but in himself specifically. The gut-wrenching cry of his very heart and soul, the essence of his being, and the purpose of his life are expressed in these words: "That I may know him, and the power of his resurrection, and the fellowship of his sufferings, being made conformable unto his death; If by any means I might attain unto the resurrection of the dead" (Phil. 3:10-11).

It is easy to understand the desire to know the "power of his resurrection." Everyone wants to have power. Believers rightly sing,

> There is pow'r, pow'r, wonder-working pow'r
> In the blood of the Lamb;
> There is pow'r, pow'r, wonder-working pow'r
> In the precious blood of the Lamb.[1]

It is natural for believers and unbelievers alike to desire power, though they seek it from different sources. And there is, of course, no greater power than resurrection power. The ability to bring life from death, to raise the dead, is uniquely God's, and Paul's desire to know that power does not seem at all unusual.

What does seem strange, however, is Paul's obsession to know "the fellowship of his sufferings." Could it be that to "know him, and the power of his resurrection" are dependent on knowing "the fellowship of his sufferings"? The answer must be, "Yes." Throughout the Bible, the verb "know" implies special intimacy. In the marriage relationship, it means sexual intercourse, that sacred physical act between those who have taken the wedding vows that join them forever together as

---

1. Lewis E. Jones, "There is Power in the Blood" (date written unknown), *Hymns of Faith* (Wheaton, Illinois: Tabernacle Publishing Company, 1980), 268.

"one flesh" (Eph. 5:31). It is no wonder, then, that Paul sought an intimate knowledge of his Lord. Did he not write, "For we are members of his body, of his flesh, and of his bones" (Eph. 5:30)? As surely as a man and wife "know" each other in physical union, Paul desired to "know" the Lord Jesus Christ in every aspect of his being, including suffering. Why? Because that was and is the only way to really know him.

In a race to determine who suffered most, Paul and Job would probably finish in a virtual dead heat. Both learned and displayed remarkable knowledge of God through suffering. Job said, "Though he slay me, yet will I trust in him" (Job 13:15). R.C. Sproul emphasizes knowledge of God as the reason for Job's trials:

> Job's trust wavered, but it never died. He mourned. He cried. He protested. He questioned. He even cursed the day of his birth. But he clutched tightly to his only possible hope, his trust in God. At times Job was hanging on by his fingernails. But he hung on. He cursed himself. He rebuked his wife, but he never cursed God.
>
> Job cried out for God to answer his questions. He desperately wanted to know why he was called upon to endure so much suffering. Finally God answered him out of the whirlwind. But the answer was not what Job expected. God

refused to grant Job a detailed explanation of His reasons for the affliction. The secret counsel of God was not revealed to Job.

Ultimately the only answer God gave to Job was a revelation of Himself. It was as if God said to him, "Job, *I* am your answer." Job was not asked to trust a plan but a Person, a personal God who is sovereign, wise, and good. It was as if God said to Job, "Learn who I am. When you know me, you know enough to handle anything."[2]

To know God is to accept his sovereignty, to acknowledge that he has the right to do as he chooses and what he chooses to do is always right, even if it involves the suffering of his children at the hands of others. Barnhouse agrees with Sproul:

If we will allow the Holy Spirit to lead us to Christ in patience, in blessing and in good deeds toward those who despitefully use us, we shall enter into greater understanding of Christ, and we will better know the sovereignty of God.[3]

Paul said in 2 Corinthians 2:14-16 that believers are used by God to reveal to the saved and lost alike "the savour of his knowledge" everywhere.

2.   R.C. Sproul, *Surprised By Suffering* (Wheaton, Illinois: Tyndale House Publishers, 1988), 52-53.
3.   Barnhouse, *Romans*, 4:85.

The knowledge of the Lord is a savour, or sweet-smelling fragrance. Many preachers and song-writers have observed that "the Christian life, like a rose, gives forth perfume when it is crushed."[4] It is through suffering, tribulation, and persecution that the Lord reveals himself to his own and fulfills his purpose in them of making himself known to others.

Rabbi Harold S. Kushner has written perhaps the best known book on suffering, *When Bad Things Happen To Good People.* Yet his own words cause considerable doubt that he has come to "know" the God of Job and of Paul, the God who inspired the writing of Psalms 22 or Isaiah 53, and the God who came in the person of Jesus Christ to suffer and die:

> I believe in God. But I do not believe the same things about Him that I did years ago, when I was growing up or when I was a theological student. I recognize his limitations. He is limited in what He can do by laws of nature and by the evolution of human nature and human moral freedom...I can worship a God who hates suffering but cannot eliminate it, more easily than I can worship a God who chooses to make children suffer and die, for whatever exalted reason...

4. Barnhouse, *Romans,* 4:84.

God does not cause our misfortunes. Some are caused by bad luck, some are caused by bad people, and some are simply an inevitable consequence of our being human and being mortal, living in a world of inflexible natural laws. The painful things that happen to us are not punishments for our misbehavior, nor are they in any way part of some grand design on God's part.[5]

This is a man who may have suffered but who did not come to know God intimately in the process. God's children come to know him in the process of suffering.

## Suffering Is a Requirement to Reign with Christ

Shortly before his death, Paul wrote to his young preacher friend, Timothy, these words:

*It is a faithful saying: For if we be dead with him, we shall also live with him: If we suffer, we shall also reign with him: if we deny him, he also will deny us: If we believe not, yet he abideth faithful: he cannot deny himself.*

2 Tim. 2:11-13

---

5.    Harold S. Kushner, *When Bad Things Happen To Good People* (New York, Avon Books, 1981), 134.

Is suffering a requirement for reigning? Can we not reign if we have not suffered? McGee believes that is exactly what Paul means in verse twelve:

I personally believe that not all believers are going to reign with Him. I believe that this verse narrows it down to those who have suffered for Him. I'd be embarrassed if I were put on the same par with the apostle Paul in heaven, because I haven't suffered as he did. I would be apologizing to him constantly for being placed beside him. I believe this verse is referring to a definite group of Christians who have really suffered for Christ. In the Roman world of Paul's day there were many Christians who were martyred—five million of them, according to Fox—because they refused to deny Christ.[6]

Revelation 20:4-6 clearly states that tribulation martyrs and saints and those who have a part in the first resurrection will reign with Christ a thousand years in obvious reference to the millennial kingdom of Christ upon the earth. Again, McGee:

The thrones are literal; the martyrs are literal; Jesus is literal; the Word of God is literal; the Beast is literal; the image is

---

6.    McGee, *Thru the Bible*, 5:466.

literal; the mark of the Beast is literal; their foreheads and their hands are literal; and the thousand years are literal. It is all literal. A thousand years means a thousand years. If God meant that it was eternal, I think He would have said so. If he meant it was five hundred years, He would have said so. Cannot God say what He means? Of course He can, and when He says a thousand years, He means a thousand years.[7]

McGee also has an explanation for where each group will reign:

The tribulation saints and the Old Testament saints will evidently reign on this earth with Christ. I believe that David will be His viceregent. The church, which is the bride of Christ, will reside in the New Jerusalem where she reigns with Him from that exalted place and, I believe, over a great deal of God's creation. Christ will commute from the New Jerusalem to the old Jerusalem on this earth. And I suppose that the church also will travel back and forth between its heavenly home and the earth.[8]

Thus, while everyone will certainly not agree wholeheartedly with McGee's eschatology, everyone

---

7. McGee, *Thru the Bible*, 5:1056.
8. Ibid., 5:1057.

must agree that the Bible establishes a link between suffering and reigning. The conclusion is inescapable: suffering is a requirement to reign with Christ. If we are to be prepared to reign with Christ in the millennial kingdom and to perform whatever may be required of us throughout eternity, then we must be inseparably identified with Christ even in his suffering.

Peter hinted at the responsibilities of reigning with Christ by referring to the "everlasting kingdom of our Lord and Saviour Jesus Christ," encouraging Christians to make their "calling and election sure" to be confident of being welcome when they arrived (2 Pet. 1:10-11). A kingdom must have a king and administrators. While believers are "partakers of the divine nature" (2 Pet. 1:4) now, which some have termed "realized eschatology," entrance into the everlasting kingdom of Christ is yet future. Christians press toward a city, as Abraham did, a "city which hath foundations, whose builder and maker is God" (Heb. 11:10). Entrance into that city, or kingdom, is only by relationship to Christ himself (John 14:6), and that is "future eschatology." The goal of the divine nature is entrance into the everlasting kingdom of Christ. Stephen experienced an abundant entrance into this kingdom (Acts 7:55-56), and Paul expected the same thing (2 Tim. 4:7-8). No doubt he received it!

In his first letter, Peter wrote of the glory associated with suffering:

*But rejoice, inasmuch as ye are partakers of Christ's sufferings; that, when his glory shall be revealed, ye may be glad also with exceeding joy. If ye be reproached for the name of Christ, happy are ye; for the spirit of glory and of God resteth upon you: on their part he is evil spoken of, but on your part he is glorified.*

1 Pet. 4:13-14

Peter, along with James and John, had witnessed the glory of Jesus Christ on the Mount of Transfiguration. The present tense of "rejoice" indicates a continuous activity, or "rejoice and keep on rejoicing." To share his suffering in this life is to be on the glory road to sharing his glory in eternity. Peter agreed with Paul, who wrote, "For I reckon that the sufferings of this present time are not worthy to be compared with the glory which shall be revealed in us" (Rom. 8:18). Paul had written in the preceding verse that the children of God are "heirs of God, and joint-heirs with Christ; if so be that we suffer with him, that we may be also glorified together." Jesus himself said that those who are "persecuted for righteousness' sake" would inherit "the kingdom of heaven" and a great "reward in heaven" (Matt. 5:10-12).

The message is loud and clear. Christians should understand that it is a privilege, not a misfortune, to be selected to suffer for Christ. The greatest proof we can have that we are God's children is that we can endure suffering for the name of Christ. There is no cause for shame. Rather, suffering is an opportunity to glorify God, to enter into a sweeter communion with him, and to give evidence that "the spirit of glory and of God resteth upon you" (1 Pet. 4:14). Indwelt by the Holy Spirit, owned by God, believers are anointed especially in suffering, even if it means social ostracism and official persecution. One day there will be great rejoicing and jubilation for the faithful when Christ is crowned King of kings and Lord of lords. What joy to be "counted worthy" to reign with the Lord of the universe:

> So that we ourselves glory in you in the churches of God for your patience and faith in all your persecutions and tribulations that ye endure: Which is a manifest token of the righteous judgment of God, that ye may be counted worthy of the kingdom of God, for which ye also suffer: Seeing it is a righteous thing with God to recompense tribulation to them that trouble you; And to you who are troubled rest with us, when the Lord Jesus shall be revealed from heaven with his mighty angels.

2 Thess. 1:4-7

In Paul's letter to the Ephesians, he wrote that Christians ought to be "giving thanks always for all things unto God and the Father in the name of our Lord Jesus Christ" (Eph. 5:20). Choosing to thank God changes the attitude. What most people want is relief, release, and escape, and most of us would choose those options. The message of the Bible is clear, however, that those options are wrong. God knows best. Believers ought to thank God even when they do not feel like it and keep on thanking him for years, if necessary. Is it possible to thank God for suffering? By all means, yes! When the child of God realizes he is being groomed for eternity and for a place of leadership in the administration of the King of kings and Lord of lords, he will thank God for the privilege of suffering for Christ.

## Believers Can Frustrate God's Will for Their Children

The young lady was pursuing her degree at a local university and working part-time to defray some of the cost. A new but seemingly dedicated Christian, she taught Sunday School and sang in the choir at the church where her father was the pastor. Suddenly, she began to have an inordinate amount of trouble with the used compact car her dad had purchased for her a couple of years previously. What had once been reliable transportation was now anything but reliable as a blown tire, a broken mirror, and an overheated engine came in quick succession.

At about the same time, the father discovered that his daughter had not been tithing her income, and there was little doubt the junior high girls in her Sunday School class knew it. She needed a reliable car, but she also needed to be obedient to the Lord. What is the responsibility of a parent to the child and to the Lord when the child is clearly out of God's will in some area? Must the parent *always* provide for the physical welfare of the child, even if it means the spiritual goes lacking?

In the case in question, the father did buy his daughter another car, but he tied a string to it. He parked the car in the basement garage and told the girl she could take possession of it when she assured him her tithes had been completely caught up-to-date and that she could retain the right to drive it as long as she continued to tithe. Within two weeks she was driving the car. Did the father in question have the right and responsibility to act as he did? Yes, he did, and parents need to know that. How do I know this story is true? I am the father, and the young lady is my daughter.

The Bible says, "Train up a child in the way he should go: and when he is old, he will not depart from it" (Prov. 22:6). The direction is "in the way he *should* go," not in the way he wants to go, chooses to go, thinks he ought to go, or believes he has a right to go. And if a child will not go in the way he should go, he must be made to suffer the consequences. Somehow the priorities have become reversed. The trend today seems to be for parents to come to the rescue of the child every time he gets in trouble. If he gets in hot water at school, it must be the teacher's fault. If he gets a traffic ticket, the officer was wrong. If he wrecks his car, buy him another one. If he wants to do drugs, there is nothing to be done about it. If he drops out of school, so what? If he drops out of his marriage, he can always come home to momma and daddy. Where are the parents today who will stand up and say, "Enough is enough—you're going to obey us and God, or you are going to suffer the consequences"? There are times when parents absolutely should not come to the rescue of their children.

But there is another way parents can frustrate God's will for the lives of their children, and that is by laying a burden of guilt on them that adversely affects their knowledge of God and understanding of how he would use them. The story of Barbara Mitchell comes to mind. Barbara was born with cerebral palsy, which affected the right side of her body, particularly her right eye, right arm, and right leg. She is extremely intelligent, bright, and perceptive, a successful school teacher and mother of two. But when she was a child, her parents could not accept the fact that their daughter was not normal, whatever normal is. So they took her to "revival after revival" and to every evangelist who came near their town in southwest Alabama, desperately seeking a miracle cure. Time after time she was taken forward during an invitation, and she had more hands laid on her and more prayers prayed for her than she could count. What happened? Nothing. Zilch. No cure.

But the solution could not be that God had made her as she was for a purpose, because surely a loving God would not let a child suffer. So the problem had to be the "S" word, *sin*. When the evangelists could not cure her, it was because there was sin in her parents' lives or in her life. And with the concurrence of her medical doctor, who never refuted any of their lies, the faith healers told Barbara point-blank, "When you get rid of the sin that's causing this, you will be healed."

What an overwhelming sense of guilt to place on a young girl! For years she tried to find the sin that caused her to be handicapped. For years she failed. And it was not until a month before her thirtieth birthday that she understood that God had made her just the way he wanted her. She experienced freedom from guilt for the first time in her life upon hearing a message from Exodus 4:10-12. Moses sought to excuse himself from going to Egypt to deliver the children of Israel by saying to

Almighty God, "I am not eloquent." "And the LORD said unto him, Who hath made man's mouth? or who maketh the dumb, or deaf, or seeing, or the blind? have not I the LORD?" God knew what he was doing when he made and called Moses, and he knew just what he was doing when he made and called Barbara Mitchell. And as she related the story to me, she said, "I want you to know that I was set free during your message last Sunday." What a shame that her parents could not accept that God could be glorified in their daughter who was less than perfect physically and so, through their blind love for her and desperation to see her whole, frustrated God's will in her life for many years. Barbara is truly one of the exemplary sufferers discussed in the next chapter.

In this and preceding chapters, it has been clearly shown that God uses trials, tribulations, and suffering to conform his children to the image of his Son, to make them yield to his lordship, to test their faith for purity, to make them trust him, to teach them love and joy, to cause them to know him, and to prepare them to reign with him. If the parents never allow the child to suffer, the child will never grow nor be refined in the fire that was likely sent his way by God to capture his attention. It is inexcusable for parents to bail their children out of trouble when they are clearly out of God's will. It is unforgivable to frustrate God's will in their lives by never allowing them to reach the position of having to rely on him. It is unconscionable for Christian parents not to teach their children to obey God. It is irresponsible to stunt their spiritual growth by removing every obstacle.

# Chapter 7

# Suffering—No Surprise

A very distraught but sincere lady told her pastor recently that she was convinced God did not love her because she had suffered so much in her life. Though she had never really suffered physically, her marriage was in trouble, and the family's finances were in disarray. She concluded, therefore, that God did not love her, though she professed to be a Christian. A careful review of the suffering of Paul and the crucifixion of Jesus quickly convinced her that she had never known true suffering. Her situation, however, is probably typical of many believers: "If God loves me, why does he allow me to suffer?" Our Lord Jesus Christ, who knew no sin, had to suffer, and the Bible teaches believers that suffering is to be expected.

## Jesus Had to Suffer

Immediately after man sinned in Adam, God announced to the serpent his predetermined means of salvation for mankind: "And I will put enmity between thee and the woman, and between thy seed and her seed; it shall bruise thy head, and thou shalt bruise his heel" (Gen. 3:15). The seed of the woman, of course, was Jesus. Peter, in his great Pentecost sermon, said Jesus was "delivered by the determinate counsel and foreknowledge of God" (Acts 2:23). Jesus himself said, "And as Moses lifted up the serpent in the wilderness, even so must the Son of man be lifted up (crucified)" (John 3:14). He also said, "And I, if I be lifted up from the earth, will draw all men unto me" (John 12:32).

But why? Why did Jesus have to suffer and die? He lived a perfectly sinless life. Why would an innocent man have to die? And what kind of God would send his Son to die for his enemies while they were still in their sin (Rom. 5:8) and would not spare his Son but deliver him up for ungodly sinners (Rom. 8:32)? Why would God pour out his divine wrath against sin upon his dearly beloved Son? The answers must be found in the grace, the righteousness, the wisdom, the immutability, and the love of God. In his grace, God gave heaven to those who deserve hell. In his righteousness, he poured out his wrath upon sin. In his wisdom, he made a way whereby he can remain God and still forgive a sinner. In his immutability, he did not change as his Son suffered—sin had to be punished. And in his love, God predetermined to forgive believing sinners. God's heart is revealed through the cross of Calvary.

The writer to the Hebrews said that Christ's suffering and death caused him to "taste death for every man" (2:9); made him the "captain of their salvation" (2:10); enabled him to "destroy him that had the power of death" (2:14) and "deliver them who...were all their lifetime subject to bondage" (2:15); and qualified him as a "merciful and faithful high priest" able to make reconciliation and to aid those being tempted (2:17-18). Christ's death certainly provided redemption from the marketplace of sin for believers as they are taken off the market and set free. The suffering and death of Christ is so tremendous in scope that all of eternity will not be sufficient to fully grasp its depth.

There is a word, however, which comes as close as any other in describing why Christ had to die, and that word is propitiation. The concept of propitiation is found in six verses in the New Testament. The noun *hilasmos* occurs twice (1 John

2:2, 4:10), the adjective *hilasterion* twice (Rom. 3:25; Heb. 9:5), and the verb *hilaskomai* twice (Luke 18:13; Heb. 2:17).[1] *Hilasmos* signifies what Christ became for the sinner, *hilasterion* specifies the place of propitiation, and *hilaskomai* indicates that God has become gracious or propitious.[2] Here are the verses:

> *And he is the propitiation* (hilasmos) *for our sins; and not for ours only, but also for the sins of the whole world.*
>
> 1 John 2:2

> *Herein is love, not that we loved God, but that he loved us, and sent his Son to be the propitiation* (hilasmos) *for our sins.*
>
> 1 John 4:10

> *Whom God hath set forth to be a propitiation* (hilasterion) *through faith in his blood, to declare his righteousness for the remission of sins that are past, through the forbearance of God.*
>
> Rom. 3:25

---

1. Henry C. Thiessen, *Lectures in Systematic Theology*, rev. Vernon D. Doerksen (Grand Rapids: Eerdmans, 1979), 238.
2. Merrill F. Unger, *Unger's Bible Dictionary* (Chicago: Moody Press, 1981), 894.

*And over it the cherubims of glory shadowing the mercy seat* (hilasterion); *of which we cannot now speak particularly.*

Heb. 9:5

*Wherefore in all things it behoved him to be made like unto his brethren, that he might be a merciful and faithful high priest in things pertaining to God, to make reconciliation* (hilaskomai, propitiation) *for the sins of the people.*

Heb. 2:17

*And the publican, standing afar off, would not lift up so much as his eyes unto heaven, but smote upon his breast, saying, God be merciful* (hilaskomai, propitiated or propitious) *to me a sinner.*

Luke 18:13

The most common synonym for propitiation is appeasement. It was common among pagan cultures, and it is not unknown today, for a guilty person to try to placate or appease an angry deity through an offering. Because of the base and corrupt nature of this heathen practice, many modern scholars have rejected the need for propitiation in Christianity.[3] To do so, however, is to profess a lack

---

3.  John R.W. Stott, *The Epistles of John* (Grand Rapids: Eerdmans, 1983), 82.

of knowledge of God's holiness and righteousness and the offense he takes at sin. These people have never seen themselves in comparison to God as Isaiah did when he said, "Woe is me! for I am undone; because I am a man of unclean lips, and I dwell in the midst of a people of unclean lips: for mine eyes have seen the King, the LORD of hosts" (Isa. 6:5).

The holy and righteous nature of God is outraged at sin and must be appeased. Paul writes, "For the wrath of God is revealed from heaven against all ungodliness and unrighteousness of men, who hold the truth in unrighteousness" (Rom. 1:18). Propitiation appeases "the wrath of God so that His justice and holiness will be satisfied and He can forgive sin. Propitiation does not make God merciful; it makes divine forgiveness possible. For this, an atonement must be provided; in OT times, animal sacrifices; now, the death of Christ for man's sin."[4]

The similarity between pagan religions and Christianity comes to an abrupt halt after the establishment of wrath on the part of God and the need for appeasement. Whereas in pagan practice the guilty party tried to appease an angry deity by

---

4.   Gary C. Wharton, *The New Compact Topical Bible* (Grand Rapids: Zondervan Publishing House, 1972), 349.

gifts of his own, in Christianity the necessary sacrifice is a divine gift. Stott says,

It is an appeasement of the wrath of God by the love of God through the gift of God. The initiative is not taken by man, nor even by Christ, but by God Himself in sheer unmerited love. His wrath is not averted by an external gift, but by His own self-giving to die the death of sinners. This is the means He has Himself contrived by which to turn His own wrath away.[5]

Both Lewis S. Chafer and John F. Walvoord prefer the word satisfaction as the definition of propitiation. Chafer writes that Christ's death was an act of obedience to the law that sinful man had broken, and that this act was satisfaction of God's righteous demands upon the sinner:

Christ in dying on the cross completely satisfied all of God's just demands for judgment on human sin. In Romans 3:25-26 God is accordingly declared righteous in His forgiving sins before the cross on the basis that Christ would eventually die and satisfy completely the law of righteousness. In all of this God is not pictured as a God delighting in vengeance

---

5. Stott, *The Epistles of John*, 88.

upon the sinner, but rather a God who because of His love delights in mercy to the sinner. In redemption and propitiation, therefore, the believer in Christ is assured that the price has been paid in full, that he has been set free as a sinner, and that all of God's righteous demands for judgment upon him because of sin have been satisfied.[6]

Glenn W. Barker makes a case for atonement as the proper definition. Concerning 1 John 2:2, he writes,

Surely the text makes clear that God is not over against man as the opponent since God is the one who sends the Son in order that as Father he may grant forgiveness to the confessor. It is sin that is the offense. It must be atoned for so that the just punishment due the sinner can be averted. The blot of the sin must also be removed so that the believer will not rest under the burden of guilt and defilement. Both actions are necessary for the restoration of the child to the Father.[7]

6.   Lewis Sperry Chafer and John F. Walvoord, *Major Bible Themes*, rev. ed. (Grand Rapids: Zondervan Publishing House, 1974), 62.
7.   Glenn W. Barker, "1 John," in *The Expositor's Bible Commentary*, ed. Frank E. Gaebelein (Grand Rapids: Zondervan Publishing House, 1981), 12:314.

Atonement is certainly indicated in Hebrews 9:5. The mercy seat in the Holiest Place was a place of propitiation. On the Day of Atonement (Lev. 16:14), the lid of the ark was sprinkled with blood from the altar, changing the judgment seat into a mercy seat. God's throne becomes a throne of grace through the propitiation, or atonement, of Christ's death.[8] The blood-sprinkled body of Christ at Calvary has become the mercy seat for sinners once and for all. When properly translated, the prayer of the publican in Luke 18:13 was not so much for mercy as for God to be propitious. In the Old Testament, a sacrifice was offered when God was asked to be propitious. Now, the publican could ask God to be propitiated because Christ had become the Propitiator not only for the publican's sins but also for the sins of the entire world (1 John 2:2).

There is one other word often used to define propitiation, and that is surety. The writer of the book of Hebrews identifies Christ as a surety by stating, "By so much was Jesus made a surety of a better testament" (7:22). The idea of surety is that of a cosigner of a note for a loan from a bank and fits perfectly in any discussion of propitiation. Just as the lending banker must be assured that the money he is lending will be repaid, so God had to

---

8.   Chafer and Walvoord, *Major Bible Themes*, 62.

be repaid before he could permit sinful man to be reconciled to him.

Boaz, under the law of the kinsman redeemer, paid the price to redeem Ruth after her kinsman would not (Ruth 4:6-10), thus satisfying the conditions of a bad note. Paul, likewise, became the surety for Onesimus the slave, writing to Philemon, "If he oweth thee ought, put that on my account" (Phlm. 1:18). And Christ became the Surety for the bad note, the unpayable debt of mankind. Willingly ignoring the biblical injunction, "He that is surety for a stranger shall smart for it" (Prov. 11:15), Jesus gladly cosigned the note. He said, in effect, "Father, put their sins on my account, my righteousness on their accounts, and receive them as you receive me." True to the proverb, Jesus "smarted" for becoming the Surety, giving his life to pay off the debt of sin.

Appeasement, satisfaction, atonement, surety. All of these contribute to the definition of propitiation, a marvelous example of God's amazing grace, and all contribute to an understanding of why Jesus Christ had to suffer and die. It was not fair to him, but it was grace to mankind. Oh, the wonder of it all, that Jesus would die for lost sinners.

## Champions of the Faith Suffered

The verses of the eleventh chapter of Hebrews sound forth the roll call of the Old Testament heroes of faith: Abel, Enoch, Noah, Abraham, Sara, Isaac, Jacob, Joseph, Moses, Joshua, Rahab, Gideon, Barak, Samson, Jephthae, David, Samuel, and the prophets. Believers of all ages have thrilled to hear and tell the stories of these champions who understood that "faith is the substance of things hoped for, the evidence of things not seen" (11:1), and

*Who through faith subdued kingdoms, wrought righteousness, obtained promises, stopped the mouths of lions, quenched the violence of fire, escaped the edge of the sword, out of weakness were made strong, waxed valiant in fight, turned to flight the armies of the aliens.*

Heb. 11:33-34

Unfortunately, the story normally ends right there, in complete disregard of the verses which follow, verses that clearly report that many were

*...tortured, not accepting deliverance; that they might obtain a better resurrection: And others had trial of cruel mockings and scourgings, yea, moreover of bonds and imprisonment: They were stoned, they were sawn asunder, were tempted, were slain with the sword: they wandered about in sheepskins and goatskins; being destitute, afflicted, tormented; (Of whom the world was not worthy:)*

*they wandered in deserts, and in mountains,*
*and in dens and caves of the earth.*

Heb. 11:35-38

From the beginning, the righteous have suffered. The first son of Adam and Eve, Cain, mur-
dered his first brother, Abel, because Abel by faith
brought "a more excellent sacrifice than Cain"
(Heb. 11:4). Daniel went to the lions' den, and the
three Hebrew boys went through the fiery furnace
for righteousness' sake. The accounts of those who
suffered in the Old Testament are too numerous to
list.

Did the arrival of Jesus, the Messiah, change
the lot of the righteous to lives of ease, luxury,
health, and wealth? Indeed not! After having
blessed Simon Peter, Jesus told his disciples about
his coming suffering, death, and resurrection.
This, of course, did not fit the disciples' image of
the Messiah, so Peter rebuked the Lord, telling
him that those things would not happen. Jesus told
Peter that he might understand the things of man
but he certainly did not comprehend the things of
God (Matt. 16:23). Then, in a most surprising and
revealing statement, Jesus told his disciples, "If
any man will come after me, let him deny himself
and take up his cross, and follow me" (16:24).
These disciples knew that the cross represented

death, and the Master was saying that discipleship was equivalent to martyrdom.

Peter and the other disciples came to understand these things of God after Christ's ascension, enduring great suffering and eventually martyrdom for their beliefs. Peter, himself, after being severely beaten, was crucified with his head downwards, at his own request.[9]

*Foxe's Book of Martyrs* is replete with accounts of Christians who willingly embraced martyrdom rather than recant their beliefs, counting it a privilege to be considered worthy of dying for Christ. Prayer, proclamation, praise, and perseverance characterized their last moments in most cases. Witnesses to the end, their deaths inspired rather than inhibited the growth of Christianity. An excellent example is Laurentius, slain in A.D. 258 under the Roman emperor Valerian:

He was beaten with iron rods, set upon a wooden horse, and had his limbs dislocated. He endured these tortures with such fortitude and perseverance, that he was ordered to be fastened to a large gridiron, with a slow fire under it, that his death might be more tedious. But his astonishing constancy, during these trials, and his serenity of countenance

---

9.   Foxe, *Martyrs*, 12.

under such excruciating torments gave the spectators so exalted an idea of dignity and truth of the Christian religion that many immediately became converts.[10]

The Lord told Ananias, the disciple at Damascus, that Paul after his conversion would suffer great things "for my name's sake" (Acts 9:16). And suffer he did. As recorded in 2 Corinthians 11:24-28, the nature of his sufferings is simply appalling. That one man could endure such an ordeal in the course of his lifetime boggles the imagination. James Smith, in what probably does not do justice to the horrible magnitude of the situation, describes:

Five times lashed, at the hands of the Jews, receiving 39 strokes each time. Three times beaten with rods by a Roman official. Three times shipwrecked and tossed in the deep, perhaps clinging to a spar for a whole "night and a day." Many long and wearisome journeys. Endured eight different kinds of *peril*, suffered eight kinds of bodily privations, and, beside all this, having the personal care of all the churches upon him. But all this tribulation, distress, persecution, famine, nakedness, and peril did not separate him from the love of God in Christ Jesus (Rom. 8:35). How

10.  Foxe, *Martyrs*, 23.

like his sufferings were to those "many sorrows" which marred the face of his Holy Master, and how truly did he thereby become a "partaker of the sufferings of Christ."[11]

Did the coming of Christ and the resulting onset of the church age stop or limit the sufferings of saints? Far from it. If anything, suffering probably intensified among believers. As so much of the Old Testament foreshadows Christ, so Christ himself foreshadowed the suffering that his followers would experience as "he humbled himself, and became obedient unto death, even the death of the cross" (Phil. 2:8). Jesus, therefore, set the tone for what would be the Christian experience until the church is taken home.

## The Bible Clearly Teaches Believer-Suffering

Despite the example of Christ and that of saints throughout the ages, immature Christians still bemoan their lot when difficulties arise and display ignorance of God's Word by questioning God's love when he allows them to suffer. In reality, the fact that we are permitted to suffer for Christ is a sure sign that God loves us. The real surprise should be that believers, particularly in the United States of America, suffer so little.

---

11. James Smith, "Suffering for Christ," in *Handfuls on Purpose* (Grand Rapids: Eerdmans, 1983), 9:178-179.

In a wonderful article entitled, "Will We Serve God When...?", Ronald Dunn asks three thought-provoking questions: (1) "Will we serve God when we are immersed in suffering?"; (2) "Will we serve God when our friends forsake us?"; and (3) "Will we serve God when God is silent?" Of the first he has this to say:

> God gave the devil permission to afflict Job. Job suffered in his person, and he suffered in his reputation, because there was a prevalent philosophy in those days that physical blessings were a sign of God's favor. So it went without saying, that if a person had an abundance of blessings and was in good health, then God was blessing him. But if suddenly something happened to that person's fortune and he lost it, and if he became afflicted with all kinds of diseases, then there was only one explanation: he had sinned. The moment Job lost the supposed sign of God's favor, people began to accuse him and to question him.

> Some preach that if we trust God, we will always be healthy and wealthy. We will be lifted above all the ordinary trials and troubles of life. That is not what the Bible teaches...

> I once talked with someone who said the problem with a particular sick person was

that that person who was sick did not have enough faith to be healed. Perhaps our problem is not that we lack the faith to be healed but that we lack the faith to stay sick.[12]

Equally perceptive is his answer to the third question:

When God finally spoke to Job, he didn't answer a single one of Job's questions. All God did was reassure Job of his own sovereignty, of his own Lordship, of his own wisdom.

The Lordship of Jesus Christ means that although I may not understand it, although I may not see the wisdom or purpose of it, God has a right to do whatever he does. That is what it means to be under the Lordship of Jesus Christ.[13]

Now, it must be clearly understood that believers are not the only people in the world who suffer. Believers and unbelievers suffer but for different reasons. Unbelievers suffer because their father, the Devil, is doing as he pleases with them. God, on the other hand, will permit believers to suffer for a purpose. Satan cannot touch a child of

12. Ronald Dunn, "Will We serve God When...?", *Decision*, July-August 1989, 36.
13. Ibid.

God without permission of God and can do no more than God allows, as is manifested in the first chapter of Job.

Both Jesus and Peter warned of believer suffering. In the sixteenth chapter of John, Jesus said, "In the world ye shall have tribulation" (16:33) and "the time cometh, that whosoever killeth you will think that he doeth God service" (16:2). That does not sound much like a health and wealth doctrine, does it? Peter said,

> *Beloved, think it not strange concerning the fiery trial which is to try you, as though some strange thing happened unto you: But rejoice, inasmuch as ye are partakers of Christ's sufferings; that, when his glory shall be revealed, ye may be glad also with exceeding joy.*

> 1 Pet. 4:12-13

The subject of human suffering is, admittedly, hard to understand, for there are purposes in the mind of God that must remain a mystery to believers for now. Suffering could be for sin and rebellion, or, on the other hand, to prevent sinning. Suffering can build or perfect character, and it can also prepare believers for ministry. Warren Wiersbe has observed that "God put young Joseph through 13 years of tribulation before He made him second ruler of Egypt, and what a great man Joseph turned out to be!"[14] In addition, "God always prepares us for what He is preparing for us, and part of that preparation is suffering."[15] As a lad, David killed Goliath, but he had to spend time in caves and on the run from King Saul before he was ready to become king himself. Elijah told Ahab that it would not rain for three years, but he had to go to the desert, drink from a brook that dried up, and eat from an empty flour barrel before he was ready to face the prophets of Baal on Mt. Carmel and bring down fire from heaven. They had to go through a time of preparation to learn to trust God in every situation; otherwise, they could not have withstood the tremendous pressure they would face in times of great crisis. God prepared them, and he prepares us, too.

Many have tried to answer the question of Christian suffering by developing lists that define different types of suffering. Barnhouse's classification includes "corrective, constructive, and exemplary."[16] Others have defined numerous types of suffering, such as judgmental, empathic, vicarious, testimonial, preventive, and educational, but Barnhouse's seems to be the most functional.

14. Warren W. Wiersbe, *Be Encouraged* (Wheaton, Illinois: SP Publications, 1984), 21.
15. Ibid.
16. Barnhouse, *Romans*, 2:78.

## Corrective Suffering

Corrective suffering is what a true child of God should expect when he is out of God's will. The twelfth chapter of Hebrews is the classic on this subject and provides one of the great assurances of salvation. Scripture is clear that "whom the Lord loveth he chasteneth, and scourgeth every son whom he receiveth" (12:6). The writer goes on to say that the very evidence of being a child of God is that one is chastened, and if a person is not chastened he is not a true child of God at all. A child knows he is loved by the fact that his parents care enough about him to discipline him, although he does not enjoy the discipline. The same is true of God's child: "For no chastening for the present seemeth to be joyous, but grievous: nevertheless afterward it yieldeth the peaceable fruit of righteousness unto them which are exercised thereby" (11:11). When we wander from God, we commit spiritual adultery—we are being unfaithful. God will apply the corrective rod to bring us back into the way that we should go. If a person can wander away from God and live in sin without feeling God's chastening, one thing is sure: that person is not a child of God. It is impossible to be his child and yet be out of reach of his loving, corrective touch. "Thus the believer can glory in tribulations that are for his correction."[17] And the

---

17. Barnhouse, *Romans*, 2:82.

unbeliever had better worry in sinning with impunity, because that is a sure sign he is not saved.

When thought is given to the great Christians of this and other times, the mind does not go to those who never made mistakes but to those who were chastened and learned from their mistakes. Chastening is part of God's refining and conforming process, for, as Walvoord has written,

> Through chastening experiences, the child of God is trained, sin is prevented, knowledge is gained, and the whole life made fit for greater usefulness. It is a maxim that great Christians have had great suffering.[18]

My father, who passed away on Christmas day in 1987, was a large man and very strong. Because of many years working as a plasterer, he had massive shoulders. Dad did not have the benefit of Dr. Spock's guidance on rearing children. Unfortunately for me and my two brothers—and my sister to a lesser extent—dad's concentration on child-rearing was directed at the rear of the child, and that with his leather belt. He would grasp my left hand with his left hand and apply the belt to my seat of understanding with his right hand. I understand the difference between a "whipping" and a "spanking."

---

18. John F. Walvoord, *The Holy Spirit* (Grand Rapids: Zondervan Publishing House, 1958), 203.

This was a whipping. Naturally, I always tried to escape, which took me out to arm's length and gave him more leverage. If only I had known to hug him. Then he couldn't have hit me so hard!

Isn't that what God wants us to do when he corrects us? Of course it is. He wants to restore us in love to fellowship. If we would be quick to embrace him and his ways, the discipline would be far less severe, but most of us heighten the pain by struggling against him and his will. In our determination to resist and escape, we turn what ought to be spankings into whippings. By the way, my dad never told me that his discipline would hurt him more than it would hurt me. It couldn't have!

## Constructive Suffering

Constructive suffering is that which contributes to the growth of a Christian. David said, "Before I was afflicted, I went astray: but now have I kept they word" (Ps. 119:67). Affliction, or suffering, played a role in his growth, making him obedient to the Word of God. Of Jesus Christ himself it is reported in Hebrews, "Though he were a Son, yet learned he obedience by the things which he suffered; And being made perfect, he became the author of eternal salvation unto all them that obey him" (Heb. 5:8-9). While many rightly have attributed this to his preparation to be the great High Priest, I must admit that to me it is a mystery and completely baffling that suffering would be constructive to the second person of the Godhead.

Constructive suffering is no more pleasant than corrective suffering, but the result is purity and refinement according to 1 Peter 1:6-9. It is good for us to be reminded from time to time that the only thing the three Hebrew boys lost in the fire was the very thing that bound them. Oswald Chambers said this: "An average view of the Christian life is that it means deliverance from trouble. It is deliverance *in* trouble, which is very different."[19] Paul said the construction project would continue until the Rapture: "Being confident of this very thing, that he which hath begun a good work in you will perform it until the day of Jesus Christ" (Phil. 1:6). Chambers concludes:

> God does not give us overcoming life: He gives us life as we overcome. The strain is the strength. If there is no strain, there is no strength. Are you asking God to give you life and liberty and joy? He cannot, unless you will accept the strain. Immediately you face the strain, you will get the strength. Overcome your own timidity and take the step, and God will give you to eat of the tree of life

---

19. Oswald Chambers, *My Utmost For His Highest* (New York: Dodd, Mead and Company, 1935), 215.

and you will get nourishment. If you spend yourself out physically, you become exhausted; but spend yourself spiritually, and you get more strength. God never gives strength for tomorrow, or for the next hour, but only for the strain of the minute. The temptation is to face difficulties from a common-sense standpoint. The saint is hilarious when he is crushed with difficulties because the thing is so ludicrously impossible to anyone but God.[20]

## Exemplary Suffering

Exemplary suffering is the hardest to understand of all the trials a believer may face, but it is at the same time the most glorious. "God subjects some of His finest children to the most terrible suffering," Barnhouse says, "so that He can manifest His glory in them."[21] Their suffering is for reasons known only to God, not because of sin in their lives nor for any perceivable constructive purpose. Their suffering is beyond the discernment of man and has to do entirely with God's eternal purpose and plan to bring glory to himself. When asked who had sinned to cause a man to be born blind, Jesus said, "Neither hath this man sinned, nor his

20. Ibid.
21. Barnhouse, *Romans*, 2:85.

parents: but that the works of God should be made manifest in him" (John 9:3). Peter said, "Yet if any man suffer as a Christian, let him not be ashamed; but let him glorify God on this behalf" (1 Pet. 4:16). Wiersbe holds that "God permits trials, God controls trials, and God uses trials for His own glory. God is glorified through weak vessels."[22] He further points out that "Sometimes God permits our vessels to be jarred so that some of the treasure will spill out and enrich others. Suffering reveals not only the weakness of man but also the glory of God."[23]

Job is, of course, the greatest example known of this type of suffering. In a nutshell, God lowered the hedge, Satan attacked viciously, Job praised God, God was glorified, and Satan lost another battle. The Bible says that when Job had lost all of his children, sheep, servants, and camels in one day, he said, "Blessed be the name of the LORD" (Job 1:21). Incredibly, the verse that follows says, "In all this Job sinned not, nor charged God foolishly" (1:22). When God allowed Satan to afflict Job with boils, Job triumphed again and praised God in his pain.

Who are these who endure exemplary suffering? They are special believers who are honored by God in this manner. Barnhouse says,

22. Wiersbe, *Be Encouraged*, 50.
23. Ibid.

I believe the Bible reveals that God chooses some people to suffer intensely, and the choice of these heroes of pain is made in two ways but with one object. God's object is to demonstrate to the invisible world, and especially to Satan, that He can hold the allegiance of those who have become His children through faith in Christ Jesus, and that nothing can swerve them from confidence and trust in Him, even though the enemy brings his heaviest artillery to bear. The choice is made sometimes at the nomination of God, sometimes at the nomination of Satan.[24]

Paul gloried in suffering, looking upon his misfortunes as marks of his Master's favor and as medals won in his battles for his Lord. He knew that if "we suffer with Christ, we shall also reign with him" (2 Tim. 2:12). Peter agreed when he said, "Rejoice, inasmuch as ye are partakers of Christ's sufferings: that, when his glory shall be revealed, ye may be glad also with exceeding joy" (1 Pet. 4:13). The joy is not said to be the Lord's. Certainly he does not "joy" in the suffering of his children any more than any earthly father would. But he does receive glory. And this glory comes when his children recognize their weakness and God's strength. The

24. Barnhouse, *Romans*, 2:87.

exemplary sufferers understand their weakness and depend upon the Lord. The Lord told Paul, "My grace is sufficient for thee: for my strength is made perfect in weakness" (2 Cor. 12:9). Paul responded with a hearty, "Amen," when he said, "When I am weak, then am I strong" (12:10). Paul was undoubtedly an exemplary sufferer.

What, then, should be the attitude of a believer when suffering comes in his life? He should seek to find out what God is doing for correction, construction, or glory. Barnhouse concludes:

First, we should ask whether we have wandered from His path. Second, we should ask Him to use our tribulation to form His image in us, in order that we may become like Christ. Then we may ask Him to use our suffering for His honor and glory. For if God can be thus glorified, and if Satan can be made to eat dust, we are delighted that God does with us whatever He pleases.[25]

In the August 1990 issue of *Pulpit Helps*, Spiros Zodhiates wrote an article entitled "Why God Permits Storms In Your Life." He said that Christ allowed the storm that his disciples faced on the Sea of Galilee to destroy their self-sufficiency and to

25. Barnhouse, *Romans*, 2:91.

make them rely on him. Though in familiar waters, they were lost without him.

The disciples were so disturbed in the midst of the storm that even the presence of Christ upset them. When they saw Him walking on the sea, they cried out in fear, thinking they saw a ghost. Your ship is also being tossed on the waves. but do not be afraid when Christ approaches. Fasten your eyes upon Him. He is no illusion; He is the only One who can save you.

When Peter asked the Lord to bid him come to Him on the water, the Lord said, "Come." Come; that is what Christ is saying to you also. Peter did not want to walk on the sea just to perform some miraculous feat; he wanted to get close to Christ. Whatever circumstances the Lord permits in your life, His purpose is to bring you close to Himself.[26]

26.   Spiros Zodhiates, "Why God Permits Storms in Your Life," in *Pulpit Helps*, August 1990, 2.

# Chapter 8

# Refining Through Forgiveness

Whoever it was that coined the saying, "To err is human, to forgive divine," certainly intended much more than that his maxim would be used as an excuse for the goof-ups of mankind. The distinct human tendency is to err. The distinct divine tendency is to forgive. But, since human believers are predestined to be conformed to the image of the divine Son of God, it is imperative that they, too, learn to forgive. The refining process is not complete without forgiveness and restoration.

Many Christians have no victory over sin in their lives because they cannot accept God's forgiveness. This is complicated by the fact that they cannot forgive themselves and thus remain under the dominion of sin. Some cannot forgive others because they have never grasped the fullness of God's forgiveness. Believers who can neither forgive others nor accept forgiveness are miserable creatures who are not only difficult to live with on earth but are also not yet prepared for heaven. Attitudes change in the fire, and unforgiving Christians may expect the Refiner's attention simply because he loves them too much not to correct this flaw in their character.

## Forgiveness Must Be Accepted in Salvation

To be saved, a person must first be lost. Jesus came to "seek and to save that which was lost" (Luke 19:10). And it is only when we come to realize that we are not righteous, that we have "sinned, and come short of the glory of God" (Rom. 3:23), and that we, because of our sinful condition, have no hope of heaven within ourselves, that we will receive the gift of God which is "eternal life through Jesus Christ our Lord" (Rom. 6:23). It is in that moment of helpless despair that the lost sinner cries out with the publican, "God be merciful (propitiated) to me a sinner" (Luke 18:13).

It is also in that moment that forgiveness is accepted on the basis of the finished work of Jesus

Christ on the cross, where he cried, "It is finished" (John 19:30), indicating that sin's debt had been paid in full forever. That is the good news of the Bible. Jesus, God's Son, came and died, was buried, and rose again. He paid the penalty that mankind could not afford to pay and defeated death, hell, and the grave in the process. Forgiveness is available for the asking.

Now, some people do not think they need forgiveness or anyone to die for them. Ted Turner, owner of the Cable News Network (CNN) and the Atlanta Braves, was named winner of the 1990 "Humanist of the Year" award, largely because of his highly publicized quotes, "Christianity is for losers" and "I don't need anybody to die for me."[1] Turner, who once studied to be a missionary, attributes his attitude to his sister's death when he was a young man. His prayers that she survive went unanswered, so he concluded he did not need a God who would let his sister die. The problem, of course, was that God could not answer Turner's prayers because he did not hear them. The only prayer God will hear from a sinner is the prayer for salvation. And Ted Turner, with all his millions of dollars, will die and go to a literal hell unless he,

---

1. As reported on radio and television and in newspapers throughout the country.

like the publican, humbles himself and accepts God's forgiveness based on Christ's death for him. It is in Christ, not money, that forgiveness is possible:

*And you, being dead in your sins and the uncircumcision of your flesh, hath he quickened together with him, having forgiven you all trespasses; Blotting out the handwriting of ordinances that was against us, which was contrary to us, and took it out of the way, nailing it to his cross.*

Col. 2:13-14

Charles Stanley, based on these verses, defines forgiveness as "the cancellation of a debt."[2] He adds,

I can say to you, with perfect assurance, that if you have trusted Christ's death on the cross to be the payment for your sins, your sins are forgiven. I don't know you any more than Paul knew all the Colossians or Ephesians or Romans who read his letters. But it does not matter. We are all condemned apart from Christ, and we can all be forgiven through Him. No matter what you have done, how many times you have done it, or who you hurt in the process, God has forgiven you.[3]

2.   Charles Stanley, *Forgiveness* (Nashville: Thomas Nelson Publishers, 1987), 52.
3.   Ibid., 53.

Sin is an impossible debt, the wages of which are "death" (Rom. 6:23), and death has "passed upon all men, for that all have sinned" (Rom. 5:12) in Adam. The debt, the death penalty, has been paid by Jesus Christ, and the debt has been effectively cancelled for all who accept his death as their payment. Forgiveness has been offered by God and accepted by all believers.

## Unforgiveness Is Sin

Who has not mindlessly mouthed by rote the words, "Forgive us our trespasses, as we forgive those who trespass against us"? This is a part of what has come to be known as the Lord's Prayer as found in the sixth chapter of Matthew and the eleventh chapter of Luke as the Lord responded to a request by his disciples to teach them to pray. But Matthew records that the Lord gave some additional instructions concerning forgiveness after he had given the disciples the model prayer:

*For if ye forgive men their trespasses, your heavenly Father will also forgive you: But if ye forgive men not their trespasses, neither will your Father forgive your trespasses.*

Matt. 6:14-15

This, then, establishes a legal requirement under the law that forgiveness be granted to others by those who would receive forgiveness from God.

165

The classic passage on forgiveness is found in Matthew 18:21-35, where one who owed an impossible debt of millions of dollars was forgiven the debt yet refused to forgive the debt of one who owed him just a small amount of money. The text is introduced by Peter, in what he thought was a magnanimous gesture, asking Jesus, "Lord, how oft shall my brother sin against me, and I forgive him? till seven times?" (18:21). Jesus' answer must have shocked Peter because it is still unbelievably hard to swallow today: "I say not unto thee, Until seven times: but, Until seventy times seven" (18:22). When the king in the parable discovered the embezzlement of his servant, the servant pleaded for mercy, and the king "was moved with compassion, and loosed him, and forgave him the debt" (18:27). But when he heard of the servant's unforgiving spirit, he "was wroth, and delivered him to the tormentors, till he should pay all that was due unto him" (18:34). Jesus concluded, "So shall my heavenly Father do also unto you, if ye from your hearts forgive not every one his brother their trespasses" (18:35).

Even had the king not delivered him to the tormentors, the servant would still have been tormented. He had not repented of his crime and thus was unable to truly accept forgiveness. He apparently did not fully grasp the situation: the debt was cancelled. The only one who was released from the debt was the king, who no longer considered the servant in debt to him. But the servant could not forgive himself, and therefore could not forgive others. He suffered from four types of torment, i.e., spiritual, emotional, mental, and physical, and his condition is typical of all who refuse to forgive.

Spiritually, those who refuse to accept forgiveness cannot have a relationship with God, as has been discussed earlier in this chapter. But even if we have accepted God's forgiveness, an unforgiving spirit breaks fellowship with God and causes spiritual torment. Why? Because unforgiveness is sin, and sin interrupts the sweet communion that exists between God and man when sins are confessed.

Emotionally, unforgiveness causes loss of fellowship with man. The person who refuses to forgive always feels that the offending party owes him something, that a debt has to be paid, and he dearly clutches the IOU in his grasp to the detriment and destruction of the relationship.

Mentally, unforgiveness eats like a cancer and causes unimaginable torment. Estimates of those in mental institutions because of suppressed anger range between 50 and 90 percent. Suppressed anger is nothing more than unforgiveness. Who has not known the experience of allowing anger to grow like a cancer to the point that the anger was way out of proportion to the offense? The more it is suppressed, the larger it becomes, and the more mental anguish it causes. It can become so large in the mind that it dominates the thinking and destroys the person.

Finally, unforgiveness can also cause physical problems if unchecked. Someone has said that "ulcers are not caused by what you eat but by what's eating you." That is good medicine for so many who allow stress and suppressed anger to eat at their insides, sap their strength, and ultimately cause ulcers or heart problems. David, before he confessed of his sin of adultery, described the physical torment he experienced as excruciating (Ps. 32:1-5) but apparently relieved by forgiveness.

Jesus left no doubt what the standard was when he said these words:

*And when ye stand praying, forgive, if ye have ought against any: that your Father also which is in heaven may forgive you your trespasses. But if ye do not forgive, neither will your Father which is in heaven forgive your trespasses.*

Mark 11:25-26

That was the interpretation of the Messiah to the legal demands for forgiveness under the law; therefore, unforgiveness was sin under the law.

Some may object that believers are no longer under the law, but under grace. That is true. And the Bible is very clear that unforgiveness is sin under grace as well. Unforgiveness grieves the Holy Spirit, as does all sin:

*And grieve not the Holy Spirit of God, whereby ye are sealed unto the day of redemption. Let all bitterness, and wrath, and anger, and clamour, and evil speaking, be put away from you, with all malice: And be ye kind to one another, tenderhearted, forgiving one another, even as God for Christ's sake hath forgiven you.*

Eph. 4:30-32

Christians are to forgive because God forgave, not because it is demanded by the law nor even because it is deserved, but because God for Christ's sake has by grace forgiven the Christian. That is the beauty of grace: it is totally undeserved on the part of the recipient. How did Christ forgive? Paul wrote, "But God commendeth his love toward us, in that, while we were yet sinners, Christ died for us" (Rom. 5:8). And his assertion, "It is finished," means he did a complete job of paying the debt and forgiving the believing sinner. Having experienced grace, believers dare not disgrace grace by refusing to forgive. Grace demands no less than total forgiveness on the parts of those who have been forgiven.

## How to Forgive

"Well, preacher, I may forgive him, but I won't forget." What pastor has not heard that line from some possibly well-meaning but misguided soul? Or, " Fool me once, shame on you; fool me twice, shame on me"? While it is a relatively simple exercise to say believers ought to forgive, it is another thing altogether to explain how.

In his deeply perceptive message, "How to Forgive," Tom Elliff says that "the secret of forgiveness is knowing we have been forgiven."[4] He described the bitterness that welled up inside him as he left for the mission field on the heels of his parents' divorce following 43 years of marriage. In Africa, his wife and daughter were involved in an automobile accident caused by sabotage. He felt a rising bitterness in his heart toward those who had caused him the pain. He felt they owed him something. It was only then that God showed him what practical forgiveness was all about:

Forgiving someone is a singular, deliberate, volitional decision by which you choose to consider a person no longer in debt to you. If

---

4.  Tom Elliff, "How to Forgive," preached at First Southern Baptist Church, Dell City, Oklahoma. Cassette A101 (Greenhouse, 1989).

that person never repents, you may not have fellowship, but it does not affect your forgiveness.[5]

I came to know the same bitterness in the wake of the divorce of my parents after 23 years. So bitter was I at their deception—they separated two weeks after I, the oldest of four children, left for a tour of military duty in Okinawa—that for five years I sent both of them anniversary cards before coming to grips with the fact I was only hurting myself. It is no easy matter to forgive and forget. "Satan will tempt you to try that person's case again in the courtroom of your emotions. Remind him you chose to forgive that person at a certain place and time."[6]

Charles Stanley agrees with Elliff that forgiveness is an act of the will, not the emotions. He lists five steps in the forgiveness process:

1. Recognize that we have been totally forgiven.

2. Release the person from the debt we think is owed us for the offense.

3. Accept others as they are and release them from any responsibility to meet our needs.

4. View those we have forgiven as tools in our lives to aid us in our growth in and understanding of the grace of God.

5. Ibid.
6. Ibid.

5. Make reconciliation with those from whom we have been estranged.[7]

Forgiveness, then, involves action. An inventory must be made of the debts for which others are being held accountable, an assessment made of those accounts, and action taken to forgive every person and every debt and to wipe the slate clean. It may well be that a person would have to ask God to show him all those he should forgive and then forgive them one-by-one as they are revealed. Just as giving thanks is an act of the will and not an emotion—thankful is an emotion—so forgiving is an act of the will also. As Stanley has pointed out, forgiveness is not

1. Justifying, understanding, or explaining why the person acted toward you as he or she did.

2. Just forgetting about the offense and trusting time to take care of it.

3. Asking God to forgive the person who hurt you.

4. Asking God to forgive you for being angry or resentful against the person who offended you.

5. Denying that you were really hurt; after all there are others who have suffered more.[8]

---

7. Stanley, *Forgiveness*, 127-130.
8. Ibid, 195.

Once you as a Christian overcome the emotional realm by exercising your will and deliberately forgiving someone, you effectively take the case out of the courtroom of your own emotions and place it in God's court. You remove yourself from the responsibility for and as a factor in the other person's behavior. Personal forgiveness sets the forgiver free from being a debt-collector. Elliff answers the question, "What will forgiveness do for you?" in this manner:

1. Set you free from your indebtedness.
2. Cast you on the resources of God.
3. Restore you to usefulness.
4. Remove you from your tormentors.
5. Remove the defiling root of bitterness.[9]

The believer who has been set free does not owe anyone a punch in the nose. You owe nothing but love and good works. Forgiveness is an act of faith, recognizing God alone as responsible for your happiness, not the other person. When you truly come to realize what you have been forgiven by God, you know you have been forgiven far more than you could ever think about forgiving someone else. Unforgiveness binds you, keeps you in jail where you are practically useless; forgiveness frees you to usefulness for God. As previously discussed, unforgiveness is torment,

9.   Elliff, "How to Forgive."

but forgiveness releases the forgiver from torment and tormentors.

Hebrews 12:15 warns of the defiling "root of bitterness." Bitterness springs from unforgiveness and causes the fruit of the bitter one to also be bitter. Forgiveness removes the root and the bitterness, returning the forgiver to sweetness.

## A Taste of My Own Medicine

I live to preach and to win souls to Christ. Because of that, my own mother does not speak to me. Surprised?

In a military career that spanned 20 years, nine months, and 24 days, I did some rather exciting things. I have visited five continents, 25 countries, and 35 states. I was a member of the elite U.S. Army Special Forces, the Green Berets. I rose from buck private to lieutenant colonel. On strategic reconnaissance missions originating in Vietnam and being fulfilled in places best left unnamed, I have been shot down and wounded. I have made 1200 parachute jumps. As commander of the U.S. Army Parachute Team, the Golden Knights, I have performed for as many as one million people at a time—that'll get the adrenalin pumping!—and as few as six in places as diverse as Switzerland and Hawaii. I had a wonderful, rewarding, and exciting career.

But lest you think I have a case of "I-tis" and am bragging on myself, let me assure you just the opposite is the case. This is a testimony to what God can do, because he was preparing and refining me in every job and in every place for the work of the ministry. I know the U.S. Army thought it was controlling my assignments, but I can now see God's hand gently shaping me for 20 years, nine months, and 24 days in the military, and even before that when I worked as a newspaper reporter. God was directing my life without my knowledge. As exciting as my career was, it doesn't hold a candle to the thrill of winning one soul to Jesus Christ.

What does all this have to do with my mother not speaking to me? Just this: the two things God did best were implant in me an excitement about preaching and a passion for lost souls. And for those two things my mother will not speak to me. Let me explain. She and a number of other ladies, most of whom divorced their husbands, banded together about 20 years ago to form their own religious group, which is nothing but a cult. Their beliefs include spiritualizing all of prophecy, ascribing Israel's covenant promises to the United States, no literal rapture of the church, and no soul winning. The last is because of an extreme view of predestination and an apparent fear that one of the "non-elect" will make it in.

I teach soul winning. I believe "he that winneth souls is wise" (Prov. 11:30). I preach the gospel of Jesus Christ passionately and invite people to receive him as Lord and Savior. I make no apologies. But because of that, my mother on March 6, 1990, severed fellowship with me, calling me a member of the "harlot church" with whom she could have no contact. A brother and sister were likewise classified and cut off.

I have never known such hurt. How could any mother divorce her children? How could she give up the joys, sorrows, expectations, or concerns of her family? Did she not realize that those with no children also have no grandchildren or great grandchildren? Is she not concerned that she will die a lonely person with no family to gather around in sickness or death?

I was bitter for a year and a half. But when I heard Tom Elliff preach his "How to Forgive" message at the Alabama Baptist Convention Pastor's Conference November 18, 1991, I made a conscious decision to forgive my mother. Our fellowship may never be restored, but I no longer hold her accountable for my happiness and have committed her and myself to the Lord. The root of bitterness is gone, and I have become much more useful. In all my bitterness, the only one I hurt was myself. I had to forgive for my sake and for the glory of God. If I am going to preach forgiveness, I had better be prepared to practice it. The medicine was bitter, but the healing was sweet. And it will be sweet for you, too.

## Restoration

Having been brought through the trials of the Refiner's fire for whatever purpose God may have had in his life, and having learned to deal with the sins of others through forgiveness, the truly refined believer needs to learn one more thing, and that is how to deal with sin in his own life. What a horrible shame it would be for him to be brought to the point in his life of wanting to walk by faith in total obedience to the Lord he loves more than life itself only to find that he does not know how to remain in sweet fellowship with God. For you to achieve your destiny of being conformed to the image of Christ you must understand and practice restoration.

As seen in the previous chapter, it is entirely possible to forgive somebody and yet not be in fellowship with him. It is also possible to be in relationship with somebody and not be in fellowship with him. Many, if not most, families include someone who does not speak to someone else. They are related, but they have no fellowship. The same situation exists in the spiritual realm. All believers are related to God through Jesus Christ. They are God's children. But not all believers are in fellowship with God, because some believers are carnal, having sin in their lives. So all believers are included in the giant circle of relationship, but only spiritual believers are included in the inner circle of fellowship. Spiritual believers can become carnal through sin, thereby moving from the inner to the outer circle. Carnal believers can become spiritual and move into the inner circle of fellowship through the act of restoration.

In his excellent Bible study on this topic, Jimmie Hefner says that "restoration involves three verbs: confess it, forget it, and isolate it."[10] Each is essential and will be discussed separately.

The great verse on confession is 1 John 1:9—"If we confess our sins, he is faithful and just to forgive us our sins, and to cleanse us from all unrighteousness." McGee explains confession:

What does it mean to confess our sins? The word *confess* is from the Greek verb *homologeo*, meaning "to say the same thing." *Logeo* means "to say" and *homo* means "the

---

10. Jimmie Hefner, "Restoration," Bible study conducted October 30-November 1, 1989 at Loveless Park Baptist Church, Bessemer, Alabama. Used by permission.

same." You are to say the same thing that God says. When God in His Word says that the thing you did is sin, you are to get over on God's side and look at it. And you are to say, "You are right, Lord, I say the same thing that You say. It is *sin*." That is what it means to confess your sins.[11]

So, if a believer confesses his sins, God is faithful (consistent) and just (because Christ paid for the sins) to forgive those sins. Forgiveness of the sins on God's part restores the believer to fellowship. As a side benefit, God is apparently also faithful and just to cleanse the confessing believer "from all unrighteousness," including possibly those sins he did not know to confess. Christians need to be quick to confess. Every believer should be as sensitive as Spurgeon was (chapter two) to his fellowship with the Father.

The second verb, "forget it," is based on Paul's personal goal of "forgetting those things which are behind" (Phil. 3:13). When you confess your sins, God forgives and forgets them. Since that is true, you have no right to remember them. This is absolutely the hardest thing in the world for most to do, myself included. My tendency is to hang on to the sins for a long time, berating myself for my

---

11. McGee, *Thru the Bible* 5:764.

stupidity and lack of commitment to God, and, in effect, doing penance for sins that God has already forgotten. It is not necessary for a believer to do penance—Jesus has already paid for the sins. It is not necessary to beg God to forgive—he said to confess. Forgetting is just as important to restoration as it is to forgiveness. Believers must not revisit their sins time and again.

"Isolate it," the third injunctive, is essential to keep Christians from becoming bitter toward God. The writer to the Hebrews warned, "Looking diligently lest any man fail of the grace of God; lest any root of bitterness springing up trouble you, and thereby many be defiled." This warning comes on the tail of the passage of chastening considered under "corrective suffering" in the last chapter. In the center of God's will, the yoke is easy and the burden light. But out of fellowship, the believer's life is hard, and he becomes weary, "feeble" (Heb. 12:12), and without strength. And although our sins may be forgiven and forgotten by God, physical penalties will follow sin, and these may cause bitterness toward God. God can turn divine discipline into a blessing when the believer submits, but discipline, like the physical results of sin, can cause bitterness when improperly received. Bitterness starts a chain of mental attitude sins and leads to vindictiveness, implacability, hostility, and revenge tactics. "Mental attitude sins are the worst category of sins and can *always* be traced back to a sin improperly dealt with in confession,"[12] according to Hefner. Out of mental attitude sins spring all kinds of sins, including gossiping, maligning, and judging, sins that condemn and hurt other believers and which are contrary to the priesthood to which believers are called and that at times intrude upon divine prerogatives. This is territory that the refined Christian should and must avoid like the plague. We are called to be helpful to our brothers and sisters in Christ, not hurtful.

The answer is restoration. The chain of mental attitude sins must be stopped at the beginning and allowed to go no further. A child has a world that is small, involving himself, but that world grows and expands. So does sin unless it is stopped. The child must grow up, and so must the child of God. We must learn to confess quickly and not to harbor sin. Rapid restoration must be our goal. It is the secret to a spiritual walk in constant fellowship with God.

## How Does It All Fit Together?

God's purpose for his children is that we be conformed to the image of Christ. The conforming process is not the same for all but is based on the

---

12. Hefner, "Restoration.".

needs of the individual believer. Christians must yield to God's will and to the lordship of Christ, and for some of us that means we must endure extended suffering. The faith of God's children is tested in the Refiner's fire for purity, because purified faith brings glory to God. Pure faith enables believers to trust God in everything, including a daily holy walk. Trials in our lives teach us real love for God and bring us joy and rewards, and suffering brings us to the point of really knowing Christ and prepares us to reign with Christ. Jesus and Peter both warned of believer-suffering; therefore, it should not be a surprise, be it corrective, constructive, or exemplary. Those who have truly been refined in the Refiner's fire scrupulously avoid the sin of unforgiveness and seek immediate restoration to the inner circle of fellowship, because the Refiner has shown them how sweet it is to walk in the steps of the Savior.

In all of the discussion about trials, suffering, and refining, one thing becomes more and more clear: God only wants and does what is best for his children. Our good is always what he has in mind for us, because our good brings him glory. He loves his children more than we can ever comprehend. What a blessed thought.

# Chapter 9

# Above and Beyond

Job may have been the first, but he certainly was not the last to be allowed by God to endure unbelievable trials and suffering in this life. I know two who have had a special place in the plan and providence of God, although I don't have a clue as to what his ultimate purpose is for them.

**Rape!**

The call was both frantic and pitiful. At first I thought it was a practical joke, because the voice was that of my best friend, and we always have something funny going on between us.

---

But this was no joke. The depth of his emotional turmoil was beyond imagination or description as he sobbed, "Brother Jim, this is David. Tiny has been raped!"

A man had come to the door of the house and asked to use the phone. When Tiny, David's wife, cracked the door open to see the man, he slammed into it with his full weight, forcing it all the way open and knocking her backward. She screamed and struggled, but he overpowered her, threw her on the living room floor, and violated her body. All the while, her 13-month old son watched and cried from his high chair.

I recoiled from what I had heard. "Not again!" I thought. My mind raced back four and a half years. David had been my minister of music and a student in law school. Tiny had come into my office in the first week or two of my pastorate, informing me that she had been raped once and attacked another time. She wanted me to know that she was working as a counselor for girls in crisis, but also that she was still working through some emotional problems of her own and might need my counsel.

Surely she had not been raped again. She was too careful. She carried a pistol. She trusted few men. Not Tiny. Not again.

But it was true. At the hospital, the woman my wife and I knew so well as a close friend was no longer a woman, but a little girl, withdrawn, ashamed, nervous, and numb. Her body was bruised, but her emotions were more than bruised: they were tattered.

Why, God? No woman should have to go through such an awful invasion of her privacy and intimacy even one time. But twice, and almost a third time? It's too much! God, how could you possibly get glory from this? How can this work out for her good? How could you let this happen to one of your children? Why, God? How is Tiny going to explain this to the teenage girls in her Sunday School class? How is David going to explain it to the teenage girls and boys in his youth choir? How is Tiny ever going to trust anyone again? How will her fragile emotions ever heal? Why, God?

The answers are beyond me. All I know is that God must have something awfully big planned for her life, because her faith has really been tried in the fire of life's trials. She has never been crucified, as Christ was, but she has surely taken up her cross. And the faith that will come out of this latest trial will be something to behold.

## How Much Can One Man Take?

Not long after I started dating my future wife, her older sister, Willa, was diagnosed as having a brain tumor. One year, two surgeries, and six months of blindness later, she died, leaving my brother-in-law with three young children.

Larry remarried, but just four years and two months after the death of his first wife, his new wife, Ruth, and his oldest daughter were killed instantly when their car was rammed head-on by another car with a drunk driver at the controls. Ruth was pregnant with their baby at the time.

He married Pat, a widow with three children of her own whose first husband had also been fatally injured in an automobile accident. Several years later, Larry himself was severely hurt and almost killed in a boating accident. He suffered a heart attack in 1991. In February, 1992, one of Pat's daughters, a nurse, died instantly in a nine-car pileup on an interstate highway in North Carolina.

Two wives, a daughter, a stepdaughter, and an unborn child. An almost fatal accident and a heart attack. How much can one man take? Larry's life is beginning to sound like that of Job after God allowed Satan to afflict him. Yet in all this, Larry, like Job, "sinned not, nor charged God foolishly" (Job 1:22). I have met few people who are as faithful to Christ and the church as Larry and even fewer who trust God as he does. He has never, to my knowledge, wallowed in self-pity but has adopted Job's attitude when he said, "The LORD gave, and the LORD hath taken away; blessed be the name of the LORD" (Job 1:21). Surely he has had to work his way time and again through the five stages of grief, i.e., denial, anger, bargaining, depression, and acceptance. But he has never become so obsessed by grief that he lost his testimony, his faith, or his joy.

All of us probably know someone who has lost a mate, a son, or a daughter, and has railed against God endlessly and blamed him for taking that loved one. What is the difference? My experience indicates that the level of acceptance of such circumstances is in direct proportion to a person's walk with the Lord and faith in him. Those who scream at God the loudest are usually—dare I say without exception?—the ones least sure of their own salvation. In the case of parents, they are the ones who have lived inconsistent Christian lives in front of their children, who have not reared their children in the nurture and admonition of the Lord, and who are reasonably sure their dead child never accepted Christ as personal Savior. They yell at God when they should be yelling at themselves.

Larry has never succumbed to that temptation. Why? He has committed his family to God. He knows whom he has believed and knows that the one in whom he has placed his trust is able to keep that which Larry has committed unto him against the day when he will again see his family. He is intimate with God, and he glorifies God with his attitude.

How much can one man take? I don't know. Why has a good God allowed Larry to suffer so? I can only surmise that it brings God glory, and "we'll understand it better by and by."

## God Knows Best

Helen Steiner Rice has written what I consider to be the perfect conclusion to *The Refiner's Fire*, a poem entitled "God Knows Best." Here's the book in a nutshell:

*Our Father knows what's best for us,*
*So why should we complain—*
*We always want the sunshine,*
*But He knows there must be rain—*
*We love the sound of laughter*
*And the merriment of cheer,*
*But our hearts would lose their tenderness*
*If we never shed a tear...*
*Our Father tests us often*
*With suffering and with sorrow,*
*He tests us, not to punish us,*
*But to help us meet TOMORROW...*
*For growing trees are strengthened*
*When they withstand the storm,*
*And the sharp cut of the chisel*
*Gives the marble grace and form...*
*God never hurts us needlessly,*
*And he never wastes our pain,*
*For every loss He sends to us*
*Is followed by rich gain...*

*And when we count the blessings*
*That God so freely sent,*
*We will find no cause for murmuring*
*And no time to lament...*
*For Our Father loves his children,*
*And to Him all things are plain,*
*So He never sends us PLEASURE*
*When the SOUL'S DEEP NEED IS PAIN...*
*So whenever we are troubled,*
*And when everything goes wrong,*
*It is just God working in us*
*To make OUR SPIRIT STRONG.*[1]

May God bless you and refine you in the fire of his love on your way to your heavenly home.

---

1.   Rice, *Loving Promises*, 15.

# Epilogue

Kaye Bailey went to be with her Lord on October 18, 1991, and Lazelle Edwards entered heaven's portals on December 3, 1991. They had fought the fight with cancer side-by-side for five years. It would be impossible to measure the impact of their lives and testimonies on those who knew them or knew of them.

Billie Oswalt departed this earth to establish her residence in the country of her citizenship on July 7, 1992.

# Appendix

# Testimony of Lazelle Edwards[1]

It is so amazing and wonderful to realize God's plan for me. The God of all grace planned for my salvation. He planned for me to draw close to Him in sweet fellowship, for His Spirit to dwell in me. Through his wonderful grace He showed me His great love for me, His care, His protection from Satan and the world, and His protection from fear and pain. He gave me peace, joy, and a desire for Heaven and heavenly things. He settled me.

---

1. Written testimony dated July 8, 1989, given to the author and used by permission.

Even though I felt some of these things at the time I accepted Christ, this experience was fuller, indescribable.

When my doctor told me I needed surgery and probably had a malignancy, I knew I was powerless to help myself. I was in the hands of the all power-ful God. With conviction, I told my family and friends not to worry, God would take care of me. I told my pastor that I was trying not to ask God, "Why?" He told me I was not wrong to ask God, "Why?" The next day I felt an inner anger, and I prayed and asked God, "Why me?" I vowed to do anything God wanted me to do if He would let me live to see my grandchildren grow up. I remembered the love and teachings of my grandmother, and she was a guide for my life. I wanted to give my grandchildren some of what she had given me. I con-tinued to pray. Now I asked God to spare me until the children were old enough to remember me.

When no answers came, I finally started to ex-amine my life before God. I thought I had been a Christian, doing the things I thought a Christian should do, but I realized it was not because I loved Him and wanted Him to have the glory. I saw myself as a small, floundering, vile thing in God's sight. I prayed for forgiveness. I prayed for His will to be done as Lord of my life. I put my grand-children in His hands and his care. I had come to the end of my will and sincerely wanted God's will to be done, whatever it took, even my life. Then I received a peace, indescribable, and then joy!

On Sunday the pastor's sermon was about turning everything over to God and receiving peace. It was a reassurance from God that He had heard me and had filled me with peace and joy. I didn't know what God's will was, but I knew everything was going to be all right with me. I had reserved some of myself before—but now God had all of me. My will was whatever He willed.

The next week was full of getting ready for the hospital and surgery. I had joy within that I tried not to show too much, because others would not understand why I was happy. I told my friends and family that I was in God's hands and He would take care of me because He does everything right.

I experienced no fear before surgery and no pain afterward. I prayed to God, "Lord, when you take care of things you go all the way. You wanted me to know You loved me, would care for me and protect me, even from pain. You showed me what grace is. I am so thankful."

When I came home, my husband and I knelt beside our bed and with much emotion we both poured out our thanks to God. I couldn't wait to go to God's house and thank Him, to tell people what God had done for me. I went as often as possible.

On my second visit to the doctor, he referred me to a cancer specialist who recommended chemotherapy.

I was somewhat discouraged, but with a determined spirit I prayed, "Lord, whatever this is for, use it for your glory, for I know you will be with me."

The side effect of chemotherapy was mostly fatigue. My husband had possibly been through more stress than I had, but he was watchful and caring. He assumed most of the household responsibilities. I went to the Word of God for strength and guidance. I was only beginning to uncover the many wonderful things God had in store for me in His Word.

I believe it was no accident the pastor's studies and sermons were from 1 Peter and then 2 Peter. I identified with the Scripture as we studied. Was I made pure in God's sight by a fiery testing? As I looked back on my life I knew times when God tried to draw me closer to Him. I was unhappy in my state of unfaithfulness, but I was stubborn! *God had to break down my flesh to get to my spirit* [emphasis added]. I was broken as I prayed, "Oh, dear God, I am so sorry. You wanted me to feel your love, and I was so stubborn." I read many of the Psalms when David was contrite before God and then the Psalms of joy and praise. I had joy and wanted to praise Him for His patience and love.

In a testimony I tried to tell the church family what God had done and was doing in my life. I felt

God's wonderful love, care, protection, and peace. I felt He had dropped a veil around me. I was His, nothing could harm me, not even Satan. Sometimes I felt I was living in the realm of Heaven.

Through the power of His Word I received a nourishment more satisfying than I'd ever experienced before. I had a thirst for His Word and the Word renewed my faith. There I found a storehouse of wealth, words of comfort, wisdom, and guidance. I found the Word was also to discipline and equip me. I knew God had shown me His love—then I asked myself about my love for Him. I prayed, "Father, I do love you. Just give me a place I can serve and show you how much I love you." I began to look for ways to serve Him, a special job He might want me to do. Surely He had spared me for an unfinished work, something special for Him! Maybe I was going ahead of God, or maybe I didn't fully understand grace yet. I began to have complications from surgery. I was very impatient to get on with whatever God wanted me to do. Two weeks bed rest, ordered by my doctor, was a nuisance to me. Through the Word, I felt God's power. I knew if I was called for something I didn't feel adequate to do, He, with His power, would strengthen and equip me. Paul said, "I can do all things through Christ, who strengtheneth me."

I visited the pastor in his office. I paced, talking, telling him I wanted to do whatever God had for me to do, but what was it? Why didn't He tell me?

My pastor, in his wisdom, watched me with very little comment. I thought, "Why doesn't he advise me? He knows something, but he won't tell me." He knew I had to uncover these things for myself. Maybe he knew I was not yet ready to accept the things I had yet to discover.

Some complications continued, necessitating a brief stay in the hospital. My spirit was high as I looked for opportunities to witness. I thought maybe this was why I was there. My pastor asked me if I knew why I was there. I thought I did, but I believe now that God wanted me to listen to Him, to "be still and know."

I continued to study the Word of God, and I prayed for understanding and ability to apply His Word to my life and the ability to exhort it to others. I was enjoying teaching a young women's class (I don't know why I didn't think this might be the place God wanted me. I guess I was looking for something harder). In my teaching, many times I tried to let the women see the experience I'd had. They reacted in horror when I told them I was glad the illness had happened to me. It had brought me to a closeness with Christ I'd never had before.

Some problems arose in the class, and attendance gradually decreased. This added to my anxiety to know where God wanted me.

I was asked to take a children's class. I asked God if *this* was all He wanted of me—just to teach children? I felt led to accept. Fifth graders had enough understanding that I could feel fulfilled in teaching them Bible lessons. Then I learned that I was not expected to teach the Bible lesson, just apply Bible truths in activities. I said, "Lord, I don't have any talent here, but I want to serve anywhere you want me to. I may not teach them, but they will know I love them."

Somewhere about that time and toward the end of the chemotherapy treatments, which were getting harder with each one, I was still reading God's Word, searching for guidance. In 1 Peter 5:10, I read that suffering for awhile makes one perfect, firm, strengthened, and settled. I asked the Lord if I was settled or if that was what He wanted me to accept. I had wanted to set the world on fire, so to speak, so that He would know how much I loved and thanked Him. He was still showing me His grace. Now I felt it. I had peace. Also, I had thought God would use my illness to influence others. Now it was as if He said, "I did it for YOU! I love and care for you, and I will be with you always!"

You may not know what I have experienced by reading what I have written, but I have had an experience truly from God, and it has changed my life, and I'll never be the same again. You may not evidently see a change, but I know I'm changed— inside. I want to keep writing, keep telling, hoping others will understand. Oh, if every person could know this Lord as I now know Him! I want to

praise Him always. I am satisfied now with a
peace, joy, and love of God beyond all I've ever
dreamed. Salvation is His gift and all He wants
from me is my willingness to let Him be Lord of my
life. I've had a battle with self-will and pride, and
it is still a constant battle that I realize I'll have to
fight as long as I'm on the earth. I trust God and
ask him for opportunities to witness for Him. I am
still trying to learn patience. Many things I am
still learning and discovering. Sometimes I want to
shout with joy and praise Him for the revelations
He gives me.

# Bibliography

*Baptist Hymnal.* Nashville: Convention Press, 1975.

Barker, Glenn W. "1 John." In *The Expositor's Bible Commentary.* Ed. Frank E. Gaebelein. Grand Rapids: Zondervan Publishing House, 1981. 12:291-358.

Barnhouse, Donald Grey. *Romans.* 4 vols. Grand Rapids: William B. Eerdmans Publishing Company, 1952-1960.

Blum, Edwin A. "1 Peter." In *The Expositor's Bible Commentary.* Ed. Frank E. Gaebelein. Grand Rapids: Zondervan Publishing House, 1981. 12:209-254.

Bridges, Jerry. *The Pursuit of Holiness.* Colorado Springs, Colorado: NavPress, 1978.

Bruce, F. F. *Romans*. Rev. ed. Grand Rapids: William B. Eerdmans Publishing Company, 1985.

Bunyan, John. *The Pilgrim's Progress*. Carlisle, Pennsylvania: The Banner of Truth Trust, 1977 rep. ed. [1895].

Carlson, Dwight, and Wood, Susan Carlson. *When Life Isn't Fair*. Eugene, Oregon: Harvest House Publishers, 1989.

Caudill, R. Paul, *Nurturing the Church*. Nashville: Broadman Press, 1989.

Chafer, Lewis Sperry, and Walvoord, John F. *Major Bible Themes*. Rev. ed. Grand Rapids: Zondervan Publishing House, 1974.

Chambers, Oswald. *My Utmost For His Highest*. New York: Dodd, Mead and Company, 1935.

Cruden, Alexander. *Complete Concordance to the Old and New Testaments*. Grand Rapids: Zondervan Publishing House, 1968.

Dartt, Tracy. "God on the Mountain." Gaviotta Music, 1976. Distributed by Kirk Talley Music, P.O. Box 1918, Morristown, Tennessee 37816.

DeHaan, M.R. *The Romance of Redemption*. Grand Rapids: Zondervan Publishing House, 1958.

Denton, Jeremiah A., Jr. *When Hell Was In Session*. Mobile, Alabama: Traditional Press, 1982.

Dunn, Ronald. "Will We Serve God When...?" *Decision*, July-August 1989, 25, 36.

Elliff, Thomas D. "How To Forgive." Preached at First Southern Baptist Church, Dell City, Oklahoma. Cassette A101.Greenhouse, 1989.

Falwell, Jerry, ed. *Liberty Bible Commentary*. Nashville: Thomas Nelson Publishers, 1983.

Ferguson, Sinclair B., Wright, David F., and Packer, J.I., ed. *New Dictionary of Theology*. Downers Grove, Illinois: InterVarsity Press, 1988.

Fischer, John. *True Believers Ask Why*. Minneapolis: Bethany House Publishers, 1989.

Foxe, John. *Foxe's Book of Martyrs*. Edited by Marie Gentert King. Old Tappan, New Jersey: Fleming H. Revell Company, 1968.

Fox, James. *Comeback*. Grand Rapids: William B. Eerdmans Publishing Company, 1983.

Getz, Gene A. *Saying No When You'd Rather Say Yes*. Ventura, California: Regal Books, 1983.

Guthrie, Donald. *New Testament Theology*. Downers Grove, Illinois: InterVarsity Press, 1981.

Harrison, Everett F. "Romans." In *The Expositor's Bible Commentary*. Ed. Frank E. Gaebelein. Grand Rapids: Zondervan Publishing House, 1976. 10:1-171.

*The Holy Bible*. Scofield Reference edition. New York: Oxford University Press, 1945.

Hunt, Dave. *Beyond Seduction*. Eugene, Oregon: Harvest House Publishers, 1987.

Hunt, Dave, and McMahon, T.A. *The Seduction of Christianity*. Eugene, Oregon: Harvest House Publishers, 1985.

*Hymns of Faith*. Wheaton, Illinois: Tabernacle Publishing Company, 1980.

Ironside, H.A. *The Second Epistle to the Corinthians*. Neptune, New Jersey: Loizeaux Brothers, 1939.

Kennedy, D. James. *Truths That Transform*. Old Tappan, New Jersey: Fleming H. Revell Company, 1974.

Kent, Homer A., Jr. *Light in the Darkness*. Grand Rapids: Baker Book House, 1974.

Kushner, Harold S. *When Bad Things Happen to Good People*. New York: Avon Books, 1981.

Laurin, Roy L. *Acts of the Apostles: Life in Action*. Grand Rapids: Kregel Publications, 1985.

Lester, Andrew D. *It Hurts So Bad, Lord!* Nashville: Broadman Press, 1976.

Lloyd-Jones, D. Martyn. *The Cross*. Westchester, Illinois: Crossway Books, 1986.

_____. *I am Not Ashamed*. Grand Rapids: Baker Book House, 1986.

Marshall, Peter J., Jr., and Manuel, David B., Jr. *The Light and the Glory*. Old Tappan, NJ: Fleming H. Revell Company, 1977.

McGee, J. Vernon. *Thru the Bible*. 5 vols. Nashville: Thomas Nelson Publishers, 1983.

McGee, Robert S. *The Search for Significance*. Houston: Rapha Publishing, 1987.

Minirth, Frank B., and Meier, Paul D. *Happiness Is A Choice*. Grand Rapids: Baker Book House, 1978.

Morris, Harold. *Beyond The Barriers*. Pomona, California: Focus on the Family Publishing, 1987.

Murray, Andrew. *The Believer's Absolute Surrender*. Minneapolis: Bethany House Publishers, 1985.

Pentecost, J. Dwight. *The Parables of Jesus*. Grand Rapids: Zondervan Publishing House, 1982.

Purkiser, W.T. *When You Get to the End of Yourself*. Kansas City, Missouri: Beacon Hill Press, 1970.

Reighard, Dwight. *Treasures From the Dark*. Nashville: Thomas Nelson Publishers, 1990.

Rice, Helen Steiner. *Loving Promises Especially For You*. Carmel, New York: Fleming H. Revell Company, 1975.

Rienecker, Fritz. *Linguistic Key to the Greek New Testament*. Edited by Cleon L. Rogers, Jr. Grand Rapids: Zondervan Publishing House, 1980.

Smick, Elmer B. "Job." In *The Expositor's Bible Commentary*. Ed. Frank E. Gaebelein. Grand

Rapids: Zondervan Publishing House, 1988. 4:841-1060.

Smith, James, and Lee, Robert. *Handfuls on Purpose*. Grand Rapids: William B. Eerdmans Publishing Company, 1983.

Sproul, R.C. *Surprised by Suffering*. Wheaton: Tyndale House Publishers, 1988.

Stanley, Charles. *Confronting Casual Christianity*. Nashville: Broadman Press, 1985.

_____. *Forgiveness*. Nashville: Thomas Nelson Publishers, 1987.

_____. *How To Handle Adversity*. Nashville, Thomas Nelson Publishers, 1989.

_____. *Temptation*. Nashville: Thomas Nelson Publishers, 1988.

Stibbs, A.M., and Walls, A.F. *1 Peter*. Grand Rapids: William B. Eerdmans Publishing Company, 1959.

Stott, John R.W. *The Cross of Christ*. Downers Grove, Illinois: InterVarsity Press, 1986.

_____. *The Epistles of John*. Grand Rapids: William B. Eerdmans Publishing Company, 1983.

Strong, James. *The Exhaustive Concordance of the Bible*. McLean, Virginia: MacDonald Publishing Company, n.d.

Swindoll, Charles R. *Living Above the Level of Mediocrity*. Waco, Texas: Word Books, 1987.

Tasker, R.V.G. *John*. Grand Rapids: William B. Eerdmans Publishing Company, 1960.

Tenney, Merrill C. "The Gospel of John." in *The Expositor's Bible Commentary*. Ed. Frank E. Gaebelein. Grand Rapids: Zondervan Publishing House, 1981. 9:1-203.

Thiessen, Henry C. *Lectures in Systematic Theology*. Rev. Vernon D. Doerksen. Grand Rapids: William B. Eerdmans Publishing Company, 1979.

Timmons, Tim, and Arterburn, Stephen. *Hooked On Life*. Nashville: Thomas Nelson Publishers, 1985.

Unger, Merrill F. *Unger's Bible Dictionary*. Chicago: Moody Press, 1966.

Vine, W.E. *Expository Dictionary of Old and New Testament Words*. Old Tappan, New Jersey: Fleming H. Revell Company, 1981.

Vines, Jerry. *Wanted: Church Growers*. Nashville: Broadman Press, 1990.

_____. *Wanted: Soul Winners*. Nashville: Broadman Press, 1989.

Walvoord, John F. *The Holy Spirit*. Grand Rapids: Zondervan Publishing House, 1958.

Walvoord, John F., and Zuck, Roy B. *The Bible Knowledge Commentary*. 2 vols. Wheaton: Victor Books, 1983.

Wharton, Gary C. *The New Compact Topical Bible*. Grand Rapids: Zondervan Publishing House, 1972.

Wheat, Ed. *Love Life For Every Married Couple*. Grand Rapids: Zondervan Publishing House, 1980.

Wiersbe, Warren W. *Be Daring*. Wheaton, Illinois: Scripture Press Publications, 1988.

_____ . *Be Dynamic*. Wheaton, Illinois: Scripture Press Publications, 1987.

_____ . *Be Encouraged*. Wheaton, Illinois: Scripture Press Publications, 1984.

_____ . *Prayer: Basic Training*. Wheaton, Illinois: Tyndale House Publishers, 1982.

Wigram, George V. *The Analytical Greek Lexicon of the New Testament*. Peabody, Massachusetts: Hendrickson Publishers, 1983.

Wilkerson, David. *Have You Felt Like Giving Up Lately?* Old Tappan, New Jersey: Fleming H. Revell Company, 1980.

Wolfe, Lanny and Marietta. "Whatever It Takes." Dimension Music, 1975. Distributed by The Benson Company, 365 Great Circle Road, Nashville, Tennessee 37228.

Wood, Leon. *A Commentary on Daniel*. Grand Rapids: Zondervan Publishing House, 1973.

Yancey, Philip. *Where Is God When It Hurts*. Grand Rapids: Zondervan Publishing House, 1977.

Young, Robert. *Analytical Concordance to the Bible*. Grand Rapids: William B. Eerdmans Publishing Company, 1970.

Zeoli, Anthony. *Why Do Christians Suffer?* Wheaton, Illinois: Van Kampen Press, 1943.

Zodhiates, Spiros. "Why God Permits Storms in Your Life," *Pulpit Helps*, August 1990, 1-2.

*The Zondervan Parallel New Testament in Greek and English*. Grand Rapids: Zondervan Bible Publishers, 1975.

If *The Refiner's Fire* has been helpful to you, why not give a copy to a friend? Additional copies may be obtained by writing to the author at the following address:

4539 Hilda Street
Bessemer, Alabama 35023

The cost of the book is $7.95 plus shipping and handling according to the S/H schedule below:

| Copies | S/H |
|--------|---------|
| 1-2 | $ 2.50 |
| 3-5 | $ 4.00 |
| 6-9 | $ 6.50 |
| 10-15 | $10.50 |

For an additional $8.00 (plus $2.00 S/H), you may order the inspiring audio cassette by Dr. Correll's wife, Dianne, entitled "Sheltered in the Arms of God."

You may find the following form helpful when ordering:

Name and address: _____

_____

_____

Ship to (if different): _____

_____

_____

| Quantity | Title | Unit Cost | S/H | Total |
|---|---|---|---|---|
| | *The Refiner's Fire* | $7.95 | | |
| | "Sheltered in the Arms of God" (Cassette) | $8.00 | | |
| | **Total** | $ | $ | $ |
| | Amount enclosed (check or money order) | | | $ |